# THE WILL TO
# SURVIVE

# THE WILL TO SURVIVE

## Three and a Half Years as a Prisoner of the Japanese

ARTHUR GODMAN

with

illustrations by RONALD SEARLE
and PHILIP MENINSKY

The History Press

First published 2002
This paperback edition published 2009

The History Press
The Mill, Brimscombe Port
Stroud, Gloucestershire, GL5 2QG
www.thehistorypress.co.uk

British Library Cataloguing in Publication Data.
A catalogue record for this book is available from the British Library.

ISBN 978 0 7524 4980 7

Printed in Great Britain

# Contents

# Introduction

This story actually starts in Changi, a small area on the north eastern tip of Singapore island. How had I come to live in this area and under alien circumstances?

The chain of events which led to my living in Changi began way before the start of the Second World War. I had finished at University College, University of London, at the end of July 1939, and had left with a first class honours degree in chemistry. While at the university I had joined the Officers' Training Corps (OTC) and had become an instructor in sound ranging, having passed all my OTC examinations. In 1937 I joined the Reserve of Officers, and when war was declared in September 1939, I was instructed to report for duty immediately.

As there appeared to be little demand for sound rangers I was sent on a short course for artillery officers, and then posted to a territorial regiment in January 1940. I did not have long to wait in England; in March the regiment was sent to France. After a period of training the war began in earnest on the 10th of May 1940 and the regiment was despatched with Third Corps to defend Belgium.

We held a defensive position near Oudenarde in Belgium, and I was in charge of the command post for one of the two batteries in the regiment, organizing battery targets. When the Germans attacked, the position was maintained for four days – with some difficulty as our guns were Mark II 18-pounders that the army had discarded in 1916 (being replaced by Mark IV guns). We were withdrawn as field gunners and became anti-tank gunners, with moderate success.

With the army in retreat we fell back towards Dunkirk, where I reached the beaches late in the evening, with about a dozen men. These were from my small anti-tank hunting unit that had lost contact with the rest of the battery. We queued on a small pier for embarking on a destroyer, but missed it by six men. It was full and pulled away – but luck was on our side because the destroyer was heavily shelled out in the harbour.

After a day on the beach at Dunkirk I joined a queue wading out to the launches, climbed aboard a small motor boat that pulled away out into the harbour and then ran aground. As the tide rose we luckily floated off the sand bank, and I eventually climbed aboard a Dutch coastal vessel. This took us to Ramsgate, where we disembarked and were taken by train to a camp to be sorted out into our army formations.

★  ★  ★

Feeling restless in England I volunteered for a draft to go to Iraq, but never reached there. At Bombay, I was taken off the troopship and posted to a regiment in Nowshera, a town in the North West Frontier Province of what was then India but is now Pakistan. I was twenty-four years old when I arrived in India – with some experience of actual fighting in a war. The North West Frontier was guarded by three army brigades, with the Nowshera brigade being one of the three. Our duties included the general guarding of the Khyber Pass and the frontier, and acting as depot battery on the gunnery range at Nowshera.

Here was my first introduction to the totally different view of life of the people inhabiting countries in the East. The range was used to calibrate guns, which necessitated an accurate survey of the intended targets. When the guns fired a safety officer was posted to the target area, as well as on the gun position. This was necessary because the local Pathans had the habit of tying their aged relatives to the targets. If the safety officer did not spot them in time, then the regiment had to pay out – five rupees for a grandfather and three rupees for a grandmother – when they were killed. This was a very different set of social customs from those prevailing in Europe.

★  ★  ★

The regiment left India after I had been with them for a few months and went by troopship to Singapore, where it arrived in October 1941 and immediately left for Malaya. Training for the different terrain now began, including altering the camouflage on the vehicles and getting used to jungle conditions.

Arriving in Malaya on 10 October, the regiment was billeted near Ipoh, in northern Malaya. On 1 December our battery was sent to Kelantan, and the other battery of the regiment and the regimental headquarters were sent to Kuantan, both places on the east coast of Malaya. We went by road from Ipoh to Kuala Lumpur, and there entrained for Kelantan, the train journey taking over fifteen hours.

The train arrived at Kuala Krai, at the southern end of the state of Kelantan, and there we alighted. The officers went to the Rest House, one of the government basic buildings for the accommodation of government officers when on tour. It was on a small hill, about 100 feet high, with a restaurant on the first floor. On the wall in the restaurant was a line about six feet high, marking the flood level for 1926, showing the whole state had been under water at that time. As we had arrived at the season for flooding this was unsettling.

The battery drove north to the small village of Chondong and waited for further orders. There was information that a Japanese convoy was off the east coast of Malaya and likely to land at Patani in Thailand, or at a beach in Kelantan. The state has a coast line about 100 miles long, roughly equivalent to the coast from Suffolk to the bottom of Kent. To defend this area was one enhanced Indian brigade of six battalions, a battery of mountain artillery, and our battery of 4.5 howitzers in reserve, a total of 32 guns.

In spite of the length of coastline, there were only two places where a landing would be effective because of the lack of communicating roads. These places were Sabak beach near Kota Bharu, and Kumassin beach, about 50 miles down the coast from Kota Bharu.

At 10.30pm on 7 December the Japanese started shelling and landing at Sabak beach; 10.30pm in Malaya was the same time as 2.30am on 7 December at Pearl Harbor. Brigadier Keys, in charge of the troops in Kelantan, informed Malay Command of the attack, who, in turn, informed the UK, who informed America – so the attack on Pearl Harbor five hours later should not have come as a surprise.

The battery set off before midnight to a position on the perimeter of the airfield at Kota Bharu, about two miles from the town, and a mile or so from the beach. We set up a gun position in a rubber estate, that being the only suitable position in an area of scrub and pineapple plantations. We could not fire because the Royal Australian Air Force planes were taking off from the airfield to bomb the Japanese convoy – with great success; they sank two transports out of three.

The RAAF evacuated the airfield in mid-afternoon when the Japanese attack made their position untenable; the battery was then able to start firing on enemy positions between the beach and the airfield, in support of the defending Dogra battalion. On the morning of 9 December the Japanese began to take over the airfield, so the battery withdrew; our last task was to destroy the oil tanks on our side of the airfield. Early that morning we passed through the town of Kota Bharu and took up a position about a mile south of the town.

The Japanese captured Kota Bharu town late in the afternoon and the battery withdrew to the first of three main defensive positions on the road leading from Kota Bharu to Kuala Krai. This position was in the grounds of a bungalow overlooking a small river, and was held for a couple of days until the Japanese infiltrated through the jungle to the back of the position. The brigade then withdrew – with the battery providing support from a series of temporary positions, using two guns at a bend in the road – in a series of leap-frogs between the three main positions.

The battery's next position was at a crossroads with one road leading to Kumassin; one battalion retreated from Kumassin beach down this road to join the rest of the brigade. This position lasted only just over a day. The

Japanese infantry could easily filter through the jungle and attack the rear of the positions. They commandeered bicycles from local shops and local people, and used them to cycle swiftly along paths through rubber estates and jungle. The Japanese High Command admitted that a lot of their successful infantry attacks, both on the east and west coasts, depended on the availability of bicycles and good roads and paths for cycling.

There were now insufficient troops available in the brigade to defeat this tactic of outflanking the second main defended position. The brigade therefore withdrew and continued to leap-frog down the road until it reached the last main position, which was defending a padi swamp, with the Japanese having to attack across the padi (cultivated rice plants). The defence lasted longer than was expected because it was difficult for the Japanese to outflank the position.

This last main position defended Kuala Krai, the railhead for Kelantan. South of Kuala Krai was a hundred miles of jungle, with numerous small rivers and swamps, and only the railway made its way through this difficult terrain to Kuala Lipis. It was essential that we held Kuala Krai while trains came from Kuala Lipis to evacuate as much of the brigade as was possible. The infantry were reduced to two battalions, with one troop of our battery supporting the infantry; the other battalions, together with supply units and the other gun troop of our battery, were put on a train. The last train drew in to take the transport, Brigade Headquarters, ammunition, and all but two of the remaining guns. These last two guns kept up a random bombardment for a couple of hours while the train was being loaded, then they were speedily entrained about midnight – a difficult task in the darkness. The train then left, with two battalions marching along the railway track, and the next morning arrived at Kuala Lipis station. It was unloaded and the battery went to a hide in a large rubber estate.

Orders were received to go to Kuala Lumpur, but as Japanese planes were active over Kuala Lipis the move was deferred until nightfall. The night trip was hazardous because the very narrow road wound over the mountains through a pass – the Gap – with hairpin bends. Kuala Lumpur was reached at daybreak and Headquarters contacted. After expressing surprise that no accidents had occurred it ordered the battery to Port Swettenham on the west coast of Malaya, about half way down the peninsula.

Having reached Port Swettenham the battery received orders to guard the coast from Kuala Selangor to Morib, a stretch of about 80 miles, with Port Swettenham roughly in the middle of the coastline. There were three places where a landing could take place with a communicating road system; these were Kuala Selangor, Port Swettenham, and Morib. Two guns were sent to Kuala Selangor, two to Morib, and the remaining four guns kept at Port Swettenham.

A battalion of the Malay Volunteer Force and a battery of guns from the Malay Volunteer Force were sent as reinforcements, so our battery was redeployed with a troop of four guns at each of Kuala Selangor and Morib. Port Swettenham was defended by the MVF. A fleet of small boats full of Japanese troops attacking Kuala Selangor was repulsed by accurate gun fire with several boats sunk; air raids were experienced in Port Swettenham, but no land attacks.

Kuala Lumpur is about 30 miles from Port Swettenham and an enemy alert was given when the Japanese started to attack it on 6 January. The town fell on 11 January, but by that time the battery had withdrawn down the main north-south trunk road. It joined the rest of the regiment at Labis, but we were soon separated. The two batteries were used to support a retreat, again in leap-frog fashion down the trunk road.

At Gemas the railway from the east coast joined the tracks from the west coast, and with the Japanese advancing down both road and railway the positions on the trunk road could have been attacked from the rear. There a strong defensive position was established, with the regiment in support. We had started the war with the regiment in the 9th Indian Division, defending the east coast. With casualties in the 9th and 11th Indian Divisions the remaining troops were united in the 11th Division, and formed the force at Gemas.

The battery fired many rounds from this position, with one particularly bizarre action. The troop commander in his observation post (OF), underneath a bungalow on stilts, suddenly became aware of Japanese troops sitting round the post watching him. With presence of mind he ordered two rounds of gunfire on the OP. When the shells landed the Japanese ran for shelter, and he and his assistant OP gunner hastily escaped to the battery without being shot at. We were then ordered to retreat because there were now no infantry to provide covering fire for our position.

The whole division retreated down the trunk road to Yong Peng, while the battery was ordered to Rengam. Rengam is at the crossroads where the north-south trunk road is crossed by the road connecting Batu Pahat on the west coast with Mersing on the east coast; the distance between the two towns is about 80 miles. The plan was to establish a front line north of the Mersing road, using the road for communications between defended positions. The battery was ordered to find a position between Rengam and Kluang, a distance of about 20 miles, south of the road, and contact the Australian brigade which had been ordered to defend the road between these towns.

We searched, but could find no Australian troops, so extended our reconnaissance to Kluang, where we found a Sikh battalion, part of a brigade of the Indian army, defending the town. The Indian battalion was overjoyed to have artillery support, so we moved the battery along the road to Kluang. The next day the Sikhs were ordered to Nyior, and we accompanied them.

Nyior is a small village, just north of Kluang, on the railway line from Gemas to Singapore; the Japanese were advancing down the line to cut off Mersing. Our task was to prevent this manoeuvre by defending Nyior.

The Sikhs and the battery advanced up the road from Kluang until the advance guard bumped into the enemy. Hurriedly taking up a position in the labourers' lines of a rubber estate, the battery engaged the Japanese and their advance was halted.

Firing began at 1000 yards, but as the enemy advanced the range dropped until we were firing at 450 yards, which is getting rather close for artillery support. While we were firing at this range the platoon of Sikhs guarding the gun position intimated that the Japanese had infiltrated past the battalion and were attacking us in the rear. We led a bayonet charge from the battery position and drove them off. The Sikh battalion then mounted an attack and the Japanese temporarily retreated again.

The battery commander had been shot while directing gun fire from his OP, and was driven back to brigade headquarters. As the enemy outnumbered us the commanding officer of the Sikhs decided to withdraw. We later discovered that the Sikhs and ourselves had been fighting a full Japanese division.* The battery retreated down the road, but not back to Kluang because that area was under heavy attack; we were advised to aim for Johore Bharu, the town on the Johore Strait, at the Causeway joining Singapore island to the mainland.

During the night the battery made its way through a rubber estate at Layang Layang, getting lost because no maps showed the roads through this very large estate. However, by dawn on 30 January we arrived at Johore Bharu, and waited there to make contact with any army headquarters we could find. We did finally make contact and were ordered to cross the Causeway, go to the village of Woodlands and await further instructions.

Eventually, orders came through to go to the village of Ponggol on the north coast of the island and to establish a battery position there. Arriving at Punggol we found a zoo, surrounded by marshy land. It was pointed out to headquarters that no gun position was feasible, so off we were sent to the Tampinis road near Changi, still on the north coast of the island facing the Johore Straits. We still could find no infantry to support; reinforcements were expected, but were not yet in position.

Further orders then moved us to Tanjong Gul, a headland on the south west corner of Singapore island. There we found the 44th Indian Brigade; they had not formed a defensive position, so we did not prepare a gun position. Instead we formed a hide in a rubber estate, and waited for further information. When reconnoitring possible OPs and gun positions on 5 January I saw the convoy of reinforcements being heavily bombed while making its way to Singapore harbour.

---

* Information from *Japan's Greatest Victory, Britain's Worst Defeat*, by Colonel Masanobu Tsuji, a senior Japanese staff officer. Published by the History Press.

On 6 January the battery itself was subjected to pattern bombing by the Japanese, with the bombs washing over the hide, like sea breaking over a beach. We had several casualties – lessened by effective slit trenches – but lost no guns or ammunition. There was still no information concerning enemy activity, or orders to prepare positions for defence. On the night of 8 February the Japanese attacked, landing in a marshy area near Kranji, a village on the north-west of Singapore island, north of our position.

The area around Kranji was defended by the Australians, and we heard the news of the landing on the Singapore radio on the morning of 9 February, but still received no orders. Listening to further Singapore news broadcasts, we heard that the Japanese had advanced to Bukit Timah village. To get back to Singapore town the battery had to go through Bukit Timah, and we now had no radio contact with all other formations.

It was decided that we would retreat to Bukit Timah between 9pm and 2am; the Japanese usually began operations at 4.30am every day. Driving at 5mph to reduce the noise of the vehicles, the battery inched its way along the road. The convoy drove through any Japanese positions – and also the positions of the British troops around Bukit Timah – and arrived safely about 3am, to everyone's surprise.

We dug in gun positions east of Bukit Timah and looked for infantry to support; on finding infantry the battery fired a few rounds. The Japanese, as usual, succeeded in outflanking the position, and we were ordered to retreat to Buona Vista road to safeguard a river position, but on arrival we were instructed to retreat to Holland Road. Having found a suitable position, east of Holland Road, the area was reconnoitred and we came upon some armoured cars guarding a cross-road. They were about to retreat and the officer in charge advised us to get into Singapore city.

The battery hastily reformed on the road and drove towards Singapore, through Japanese troops taking up positions on one side of the road and British troops on the other. Luck held, and the battery, going about 50mph, escaped with only a few bullet holes through the trucks. Continuing on, the battery arrived at the sea front and took up a position on Beach Road, with the gun trails in the monsoon drain at the side of the road. A command post was established in Raffles Hotel, obliquely in front of the guns.

The British forces formed a perimeter around Singapore city in the shape of a semicircle, with both ends at the sea front. A battalion of the Malay Regiment defended a position at Pasir Panjang, a strip of land on the western end of the perimeter. This position had its back to the sea and stuck out of the perimeter like a long finger. In the afternoon the acting battery commander found the Malay battalion and offered support, which was gratefully accepted. The date was 12 February and it was late afternoon when the battery became heavily engaged with prolonged firing. In spite of repeated attacks the Malay battalion held firm and refused to withdraw from its position.

Friday, 13 February was a day of constant attacks, accompanied by heavy bombing and shelling. Water was running short in Singapore city as the reservoirs and the pipe line from Johore had been captured. By the morning of 15 February, Lieutenant-General Percival, the Commander-in-Chief of the Malayan Forces, had decided that further resistance was not possible, and negotiations for surrender were started.

The command was received by the battery that hostilities would cease at 4pm on the 15th, and at 3pm the last order was given for 43 rounds of gun fire on Racecourse Village. The ammunition was now completely expended so the gunners removed the nuts on the recoil mechanism of the guns; if the guns were fired they could explode. This task was completed just before the ceasefire.

The battery joined the rest of the regiment and settled down for the night of 15 February on the sea side of the Padang, the open space at the centre of Singapore. On the morning of 16 February the guns and vehicles were parked in a field near Tanglin, and the battery marched off to captivity at Changi, carrying whatever belongings we could manage on a twenty-mile walk.

The long march to Changi ended the first night at a small village, called Tanah Merah, where RAF personnel had been billeted. We went thankfully into the empty huts, with a lot of overcrowding, and settled down to sleep. The next day some food was organized and we looked at our surroundings – a village near the sea shore on the eastern side of Singapore island, about a mile short of Changi. The day passed uneventfully checking on all ranks to see whether the stragglers had arrived safely.

The next night was interrupted by some rifle fire and other explosions, making us wonder whether the capitulation had been completed. In the morning, after a meal, we explored the sea shore, not seeing any Japanese in the vicinity. At the other end of a shallow bay we saw a 'bunch' of Chinese, roped together, all dead. The bodies looked like a bundle of firewood, and appeared to have been machine-gunned while roped together. The corpses were lying against each other, some just off the ground, but most of them slumped down, some almost on their knees.

The Japanese hated – and feared – the Chinese, so had apparently lost no time in rounding up all those they suspected of being able to make some form of resistance. It was puzzling as to why these Chinese had been roped together before execution, but we presumed it was the quickest method of dealing with a mass execution. As we thought we could see Japanese soldiers near the dead Chinese, we decided a closer inspection was unwise.

With hands bound, and roped together, the Chinese would have been unable to escape the rounds from a machine gun; they could not run away, as they all faced in different directions. Those in the centre of the bunch were immobilized by those at the edge who had been killed first. One could imagine the thoughts of those in the centre of the group, when those on the outside were being shot, while they on the inside could do nothing to evade the bullets. As far as we could see from a distance, none were left alive. The tide was rising and lapping over the feet of those nearest the sea.

Shortly after this unpleasant experience the regiment was paraded and on its way to Changi, where we were imprisoned in Changi Gaol. The sight of the execution had raised doubts about our own fate; we could only guess at the reasons for the execution of the Chinese and feared the Japanese might deal with us in the same manner. As it turned out this was not the case, only POWs attempting to escape were in danger of execution when caught.

# Interlude

The description of the campaign in Malaya, and of my previous experiences, can be viewed through Western thought which has a set of rules for conduct, for both peace time and war time. Both British and Indian soldiers followed these rules. The ensuing description of life under the Japanese has to be viewed through Eastern thought, as explained below.

Whenever POW and Japanese are associated in British minds, the words 'torture' and 'brutality' are recalled by the majority of people. Torture implies the infliction of intense pain for revenge, cruelty, or to extract information; only the latter is really applicable to POWs, since the Japanese adhered to the POW conventions of the 1907 agreement. The Japanese had no need to interrogate POWs on military information, as it was no longer relevant. Escape was a subject for interrogation for the very few who attempted it, as the nearest friendly territory was either 2000 miles north of Thailand, or 3000 miles south, and none succeeded in reaching safety. Clandestine radio sets, and broadcast information, were the main object of POW interrogation, and members of signal units were prime subjects for questioning. For most POWs, however, interrogation was rarely seen, or heard of.

Brutality is subject to a wide interpretation, both historically and globally. In Britain, views on brutality have changed over the years; it is only just over 120 years ago that flogging in the British army was abolished, and Queen Victoria wondered how discipline could be maintained, as it was then considered a normal punishment. The Korean and Taiwanese guards were mainly responsible for any brutality suffered by POWs on the Burma-Siam railway, but the ill-treatment of Asian coolies working on the railway was far worse and has rarely been mentioned. The majority of British prisoners in Thailand came from 18 Division, whose troops had no experience of Eastern thought and customs, so judged their treatment by Western standards. This is probably the reason why brutality has been the subject of much sensationalism.

No Japanese soldier considered surrendering, as if he did, he could no longer return to his town or village and maintain his honour. The number of Japanese taken prisoner was very small and, in 1945, many Japanese soldiers were doubtful about surrendering, even though the Emperor had commanded it.

This coloured the Japanese view of British POWs, considering such soldiers beneath contempt. The Japanese also held the Indian National Army (INA) in contempt as turncoats, and still hold the Koreans and Taiwanese in contempt as members of an inferior civilization, so all three were used as guards for the POW camps in a contemptuous gesture. The INA were used as guards in Changi, and rarely interfered with POWs. The Koreans and Taiwanese were ill-treated by the Japanese and passed on the treatment to the prisoners. Few Japanese soldiers had contact with POWs in Thailand, and had even less contact in Changi.

The outlook of people in Asia differs from that in the West, because the East deems the community more important than the individual. The standing of an individual in a community is determined by an Asian quality best translated as 'face'. To lose face is to lose respect and attract contempt in a community. When a Japanese soldier slapped the face of a Korean guard, the action was not a physical punishment, but a cause of a loss of face in the presence of POWs. To attempt to regain face, the guard had to demonstrate his superiority over the POWs by a brutal act on more than one POW. Such brutality was not particularly aimed at an individual, but at the community of POWs. At all cost, whatever the action, an Asian must preserve face.

The Chinese have a proverb: 'ride tiger, no dismount', best rendered into English as 'He who rides the tiger can never dismount', and this was very applicable to the situation in South East Asia. Britain rode the tiger all over the East, from India to China, but dismounted when Singapore fell. There was a gleeful Asian reaction to Singapore's collapse, and the normal Eastern reaction to a defeated opponent is to kick him hard when he is down, i.e. the tiger's revenge. There was a strong element of this reaction in the Asian treatment of European prisoners, a point not always noted in contemporary thought. This reaction surfaced in the Dutch East Indies, when the Japanese, after the surrender at the end of the war, told the Indonesians that Asians had defeated Europeans, so continue the struggle. The result was the formation of Indonesia, as the Dutch were too weak to combat an insurrection. Not hitting an opponent when he is down is considered a sign of weakness in Asia.

The description of POW life in Thailand that follows has not emphasized, or drawn attention to, the treatment of POWs, as it is necessary to bear in mind the above observations when forming an opinion on brutality and torture said to have been inflicted on POWs in S.E. Asia. Civilians are not included in the description of captivity, because their treatment by the Japanese has been described in other books.

★  ★  ★

The country now called Thailand was known before World War II as Siam. In the book either term has been used depending on the circumstances, to describe factual events in what was Siam. The people are always referred to as Thais.

# CHAPTER I

# We say welcome to sunny Singapore

In Changi, after three moves in a week, the regiment settled into army huts in the prison camp, and remained there for the next six months. The time passed very slowly.

As the regiment maintained military discipline, the colonel decided that the Regimental Mess should have a proper mess night, once a week. Thursday was chosen for the night and officers from other units were invited, on a scale of four guests per week for the colonel, two per week for majors, one per week for captains, and one per month, if they were lucky, for subalterns. The Japanese gave a ration of 10 cigarettes per week to each officer, and one cigarette had to be handed in to form a prize for mess night. After dinner we played whist, usually with fancy rules, to see who would get the prizes. Many enemies were made by rash play – with 20 cigarettes at stake for the first prize.

I had a major part to play in this weekly fun, as I was Mess Secretary, and had to devise special dishes from the somewhat limited rations. The regiment had a wood party, consisting of an officer carrying a flag announcing the fact we were POWs seeking wood for fires; I always went on this wood party, trying to find anything edible that would improve the mess dinner. The party had the usual stripped-down lorry chassis, hauled by a dozen men; whilst collecting wood I looked out for food. On one trip I saw a tree with fruit in the shape of a bean, so I took a specimen, cut it open, and decided it was tamarind. When I returned to the camp, I looked up Corner's *Wayside Trees of Malaya* to confirm that it was, having studied the leaves and fruit, indeed, a tamarind tree. Tamarind is a dark brown, fleshy pulp with a tart, fruity taste. On the next trip, we picked enough fruit to form a pudding, and the cook went into ecstasies at the thought of a tamarind tart. The tart was duly made and served with a flourish at dinner.

Everybody in the Mess enjoyed it, and the colonel said: 'Damned good tart, that: haven't enjoyed a tart so much for a long time. Good show.' The evening was a great success, although I had a partner whose attempts at whist were abysmal, and no cigarettes came my way.

About midnight I awoke with a ghastly stomach ache, and made a quick dash for the lavatories. There I fell in behind the colonel and all the officers from the Mess. The colonel said, tersely: 'That damned tart, find out what it was.'

The next wood trip found me searching for the tree, which I located and collected fruit and leaves. I took these to Southern Area, where the local Volunteer Units had people who had been members of the Agricultural Department in Malaya. I showed them what I had collected, and they eagerly inquired whether I could supply the camp with more of the fruit. I said I could but why did they want it? They replied that the hospital would require a lot; it was cascara, a good old-fashioned purgative. I wondered what the Mess would think when they found that they had been fed on cascara, but at least the doctors were happy. I did find out, also, that it required an expert botanist to distinguish between tamarind and cascara, so that put my mind at rest.

The dull, uneventful camp life was broken one day by the new Japanese commander, General Fukuye Shimpei, announcing that all ranks had to sign an undertaking that they would not escape. This was contrary to the international code for prisoners of war, and all ranks were told to refuse the Japanese order. When the General was told of the refusal he took action which surprised the camp. We were ordered to pack up our belongings, load them on to our wood-collecting trucks and march to an army barracks about a mile away. This was Selarang Barracks, previously used to house a battalion of British troops, but now all the POWs were packed into the one barracks. This consisted of a hollow square, with buildings around three sides of the square, which before had been the parade ground, covered in tarmac, for the battalion.

A road ran round the barracks, and our trucks were left on the other side of the road, while we were made to enter the barrack blocks. Japanese guards covered the road with machine guns, so that once separated from the trucks we could not go back to them. In the buildings, which had three storeys, each person was allotted a small space, about five feet by one and a half feet, hardly enough room for sleeping. The first necessity was the provision of lavatories, and these were dug as holes off the parade ground, with a rough cover, in some cases, of a canvas screen. Very soon queues formed and as time wore on it took about half an hour to work through the queue to a lavatory. One always seemed to get on the slowest queue, and there was much rude muttering. One private remarked, as he was retiring behind a screen, that he wished his sergeant-major could see him now – he had always wanted to do just that on the parade ground.

Food, of sorts, was made available, but conditions slowly became intolerable. The Japanese repeated their demand, but it was again refused. After a day or so the Japanese threatened that if we did not sign, the space we occupied would be halved every day. After a lot of consultation and as symptoms of illness became apparent amongst the prisoners (an outbreak of diphtheria), a decision was taken to sign, emphasising that the signatures had been made under duress. This was done, and thankfully we returned to what had now become the luxury of our old huts.

About the middle of summer 1942 an event occurred that gained the regiment a certain amount of notoriety. On a very ordinary day a fatigue party was called to fall in under the command of the sergeant-major. An altercation took place on the parade, although the origin of the words that started the event did not seem entirely clear to the rest of the regiment. However, the sergeant-major reported to the duty officer that the men were refusing to obey a command. This was passed on to the colonel, who decided that an incipient mutiny was threatened and after that events moved fast.

Most of the regiment were completely unaware of what had happened and what was happening. The colonel called for a court-martial, and one was duly convened. Rumours reached us but we had no firm information. The court-martial was held and some of the men who had been on that parade were judged guilty of disobeying a lawful order. Varying sentences of imprisonment were imposed and quickly promulgated. The regiment fell in on parade in a hollow square, the sentences were read out, and the prisoners marched off under an escort of military police. As far as we knew the police formed a military prison inside the POW camp, and the prisoners served their sentences there. To anticipate the remainder of this story, when we returned from Siam there was no trace of the military prison, and no news of the fate of the men – no information on the subject at all.

In October 1942 most of the regiment was transported to Japan and even farther afield, indeed one of my friends ended up working in a salt mine in Mukden in Manchuria. This left about 170 officers and men in Changi, and as time went on further small drafts were taken away and sent to other parts of the Japanese-occupied territories.

We, the final remnants of the regiment, had arrived in Changi village about the end of 1942. The date was uncertain for we had little means of marking the passing of time; every day was the same since Sunday had ceased to be observed as a day of rest. This was not abnormal because both the Chinese and Japanese use a month as the measurement of time and there is no equivalent of a week. The Chinese celebrate the second day of the second month, the third day of the third month and so on, a useful way to get work done. It eliminates the western weekend and the concept of a poet's day.

We were now down to a strength of 80, the final remnants of the regiment, and were organized as a battery in our particular area.

★   ★   ★

It is evening and tranquillity is about to descend on Changi village. Twilight in the tropics lasts for only about ten minutes, going from full daylight to complete darkness in that time. Just before, during, and just after this period there is a hush in the world.

The air is perfectly still, smoke from wood fires ascends lazily and sounds appear magnified. A conversation at a normal level can be heard up to a quarter of a mile away and even further in the valley. There are no animal noises, the daylight contingent is settling down for the night and the nocturnal contingent has not yet woken.

A metalled road runs through the village, bordered on each side by a wide grass verge on which tall, leafy angsana trees are growing to give shade. Behind the verges, on both sides of the road, are several rows of wooden Chinese shophouses, spread out alongside the verges.

A shophouse consists of an open room with a concrete floor. The front is protected by a low wooden wall with posts supporting an upper storey in which are bedrooms for the shopkeeper's family. Below, at the back of the shop, there is a concrete kitchen and wash place, the latter doubling as a lavatory. In the wash place is a square concrete tank, waist-high and tiled. The tank is filled with water from a tap and a dipper is used in bathing for throwing water over yourself.

At the back of the shophouses are several rows of coolie quarters – government property built of concrete with tiled roofs. In 1943 one of the shophouses was used as the battery office, sparsely furnished with only a table and a bench. The regiment had consisted of two batteries, whereas most regiments were organized into three batteries. Each battery had eight howitzers, guns capable of firing at a high elevation for low ranges to a target. The Changi office was the headquarters of the battery and it held all the records of pay, sick personnel, and the distribution of food; there was little else for which to keep records.

★   ★   ★

Peter Piper and I shared a coolie quarter. Peter was a lieutenant in a Jat battalion with the 45th Indian Brigade which was sent to defend the Muar River on the west coast of Malaya, part of the main defence of the State of Johore. The Japanese attacked down the river towards its mouth, while, at the same time, sending a force in small boats along the coast to attack the rear of the defensive position. After confused fighting the brigade withdrew southwards and was reinforced by two Australian battalions.

The withdrawal took the brigade south to Batu Pahat, with a defensive position on the river by the town. This position was overrun by the Japanese, and the Indian Brigade destroyed. Peter, with a few Indian soldiers, escaped and made their way to Rengam.

At Rengam, the main north-south trunk road crosses the road joining Batu Pahat to Kluang, and to Mersing on the east coast of Malaya. In the

Rengam area Peter met up with British troops, including our other battery, and retreated with them to Johore Bharu, and thence to Singapore. As there were no other surviving officers of Peter's battalion, he joined our regiment in Changi, and finally came to Changi village with me.

★   ★   ★

In the twilight of the evening we used to sit on the porch where we had a couple of chairs and a *kerosi panjang*. This is a wooden chair, rather like a deck chair but with arms. Instead of canvas the seat is made of wood slats connected by string, so it takes up your shape when you sit in it. The arms have extensions which swivel to any angle, usually straight out in front. You drape your legs over the extensions and sit with arms and legs akimbo. The chair is especially suited to the tropics because air flows over your whole body and gets to the parts other chairs cannot reach. As we had only one *kerosi panjang*, we each sat in it on alternate days – with Sunday reserved for guests.

Coolie quarters were government quarters Class 12, the lowest grade of accommodation. They were reserved for menial staff – such as labourers in government service – who were given the quarters free of charge.

Each quarter was roughly divided in three, with a large porch at the front, a room in the middle, and an enclosed small yard at the back. The middle room had a big plank platform – the sole article of furniture – which served as a bed and table. We slept on this platform, which was covered with a rush mat, as had the original occupants. It was not ideal for sleeping but apparently had been good for the fecundity of the pre-war occupiers.

The yard had a covered way with a concrete table; this was used for cooking, with concrete raised portions to hold a pot and with a fire underneath. A small bathroom with a tap was used for washing and sanitary purposes. The covered way and the bathroom surrounded a small courtyard about eight feet by six feet. Friends from other regiments used to visit us and comment on the comparative luxury in which we lived.

At the start of the Japanese invasion the regiment had been in the 9th Indian Division, but when that division was eliminated the regiment had been transferred at Gemas to the 11th Indian Division. When the POW camp was formed each individual command was allocated a particular area. Together with all other Indian army units, the regiment was accommodated in the 11th Indian Division area.

The Indian other ranks were put in camps away from Changi, so only the British officers of these units were in the area. Our regiment was entirely British so we were one of the few units with officers and other ranks together. The other areas of the POW camp were the 18th British Division area, the Australian area, the hospital area and Southern area. Southern area accommodated the volunteer forces of Singapore and Malaya.

To get a picture of the entire POW camp imagine a triangular piece of land jutting out to a headland which was called Changi Point. This head land is at the north-east corner of Singapore island, about twenty miles from Singapore town. Along the northern coast was the Tampinis road and along the eastern coast was Changi road which lead to Changi village. The village was about half a mile from Changi Point, on the Changi road.

The base of the triangle ran from the eastern coast to the northern coast and was marked by a continuous line of barbed wire entanglements, with an entrance on the Changi road. This entrance was about two hundred yards from Changi Gaol, with the gaol outside the POW camp. Each of the camp areas was also enclosed in a ring of barbed wire with a guard hut at the entrance. The areas were connected by the existing road system.

Should you visit the area now you would find the road system has been completely changed and Changi village has many large concrete buildings. In a small museum next to Changi Gaol there is a map of the original POW areas, for comparison with the present layout.

# CHAPTER II

# We'll never get off the island

Our billets in Changi village were in Southern area which measured about one mile by half a mile. The area contained several little conglomerations of buildings, old army and naval quarters and small hamlets from which the original inhabitants had been displaced. It was thus possible to walk round the area and visit other army units, but prisoners were not allowed to go out of the area except under special circumstances.

The guards were mainly Indian soldiers who had joined the Indian National Army, formed by the Japanese. Japanese soldiers conducted the roll calls and administered the working parties but that was the only time that the Japanese came into the area; the Indians never did. There was an exception and that was the *Kempei-tai*, a branch of the Japanese army that was roughly equivalent to the Gestapo. These gentlemen had black triangles on the sleeves of their uniform and were usually seen cycling round an area and between the areas. Both Japanese and Indian troops were distinctly afraid of these men.

The battery had four officers, three of whom were gunners and the fourth was Peter Piper who shared the coolie quarter with me and who came from a battalion of the Jats.

Peter and I had a small garden in front of the coolie quarter that we shared, and in it we grew vegetables for ourselves and for the chickens we kept. The soil was poor so we adopted the Chinese practice of using night- soil. Urine is collected throughout the night and day and put on the garden after dark.

In villages in mainland China, there was always a large earthen tong or jar, about four feet high, with a platform around it so that the farm labourers could provide a 'specimen' on their way to and from work. Nightsoil is a precious commodity in China and also used to be collected in Malaya and sold to the farms. It is an excellent form of manure and our garden plants thrived on it.

The use of nightsoil is a true form of conservation because little is lost from the nitrogen cycle and compares very favourably with the losses incurred by dumping sewage out to sea. The Chinese, with a quarter of the world's population and a small fraction of the world's cultivatable surface, have had to discover the most efficient means of producing food. The use of nightsoil solved the fruit and vegetable situation and the animal protein situation was solved by raising pigs and ducks, the fastest throughput of animal protein from the available land.

The eggs we obtained from the hens and ducks were made into omelettes and supplemented the normal diet of rice and vegetables. Our quarter was one of eight or so in a row of quarters and the other quarters each had two officers installed in them. Each quarter had its own little garden and everybody grew their own produce.

We also tried to grow fruit, the obvious choice being papaya which had a rapid growth rate to the first fruiting. We planted three seeds and hoped for the best, but Murphy's law intervened. Two seeds died and the third produced a male tree with beautiful, heavily-scented flowers but useless as it had no fruit. This reminded us of Donovan's law – Murphy was an optimist. Time was to prove too short to experiment with other fruit trees of which Malaya has a surprisingly great variety.

All ranks received the same rations of food from the Japanese, consisting of rice and vegetables. The diet produced many vitamin deficiency diseases with beriberi the main scourge. Beriberi causes a slow deterioration of the nervous system, giving rise to a condition known as 'happy feet' in which it was not possible to raise the feet when walking, thus producing a shuffling gait and, in extreme cases, only the ability to crawl along with the aid of a stick.

The first signs of beriberi appear when the hairs on your leg are pulled and nothing is felt. Rice polishings (bran) and red palm oil were used to cure the disease, with the cure being almost as bad as the disease. Lack of vitamin A, owing to a lack of animal products and red-coloured fruit and vegetables, produces mosaic vision in which the retina of the eye is destroyed in small patches. Once again red palm oil came to the rescue.

As officers and, perhaps temporary, gentlemen, the Japanese gave us the pay of the equivalent Japanese rank, irrespective of whether the officer was working or not. In my case this amounted to 250 yen per month. The Japanese then proceeded to charge for accommodation and food and 90 yen a month for paper.

The paper ration was a full copy of the *New York Times* per month. This is a large paper and was normally sufficient for all purposes, but a heavy smoker ran into difficulties if he had diarrhoea and, consequently, had to take a few agonizing decisions.

Eventually we came to know so much about paper manufacture that a page of the paper could be split into two, providing much more suitable cigarette paper than the original. The local inhabitants used to form a small, thin pyramid of paper, put the tobacco in the pyramid, and then hold the top of the pyramid in their mouth so that little tobacco was wasted at the end of the smoke. We preferred a more conventional cigarette.

A ration of ten cigarettes per week was given to all ranks and the five per cent of non-smokers carried out a lively trade for their cigarette ration. Also popular were cheroots – either Burma or Java cheroots – which were very cheap; a bundle of 20 Burma cheroots cost only 50 sen – half a yen. The Burma cheroots were about two inches long, somewhat pyramidal in shape, very black, and giving out a powerful odour when smoked. The troop's nickname for them was 'nigger's pricks'.

I did not receive the balance of my 250 yen per month. After the Japanese deductions I was left with thirty yen, of which the Malayan Command took ten yen to provide food for the other ranks in hospital. The Japanese worked on the theory that if they neither paid nor gave food to the sick, then the sick were encouraged to get better more quickly.

As I was a gunner, the Artillery organization deducted a further ten yen to provide amenities for sick gunners in hospital, leaving me with ten yen. All this was duly recorded and Malayan Command said we would have the money refunded on our release.

Under military convention the British government would pay the Japanese government for our emoluments. At this stage of our captivity ten yen was a fair sum of money and enabled us to buy odd fruit, coconuts, tobacco and sweets, but no meat or fish.

The men, NCOs, and warrant officers were paid only when they worked, but they received the same rations as the officers whether they worked or not and also the ration of 10 cigarettes per week.

The rations were purchased by members of the Volunteer Forces who had worked in Malaya before the war and who were proficient Malay speakers, used to dealing with local business men. The purchasing was under the control of Japanese personnel who arranged payment for the produce.

Distribution of the food was carried out in the same manner. The army cooks became very experienced in presenting the rice and vegetables in a variety of new dishes. Special efforts, such as pies, were given the universal name of 'doovers' – believed to have originated in the Australian area as the closest approach to 'hors-d'oeuvres'. The food was distributed by the cooks under supervision of the NCOs and watched with hawk-like eyes by all the recipients. Nothing provoked anger more than what was considered an unfair distribution of food. We were all trained in the same way and even now an ex-POW can look at a plate of cakes and select the largest without hesitation. Semi-starvation proved an excellent teacher.

Men who were very sick were transferred to the hospital area where the hospital was accommodated in an old army barracks. Not many were transferred from the unit areas as each unit had its own doctor who treated the sick on a daily basis. The hospital contained all the wounded from the fighting during the campaign. Those that became fit were transferred back to their units.

This still left a considerable number of officers and men who had suffered amputation of limbs or other serious injuries. The men in these conditions in the hospital received neither pay nor rations, following the Japanese custom of not feeding sick personnel. This was the reason why each officer contributed ten yen of his pay to provide food for the inmates.

Drugs were in short supply, and mainly confined to hospital use, with little left over for use by unit medical officers. The majority of the diseases suffered by POWs were due to vitamin deficiencies in the diet, mainly deficiencies in vitamin A and the B group of vitamins.

One vitamin B deficiency caused the skin of the scrotum to slough off, an affliction known colloquially as 'Changi balls'. The standard cure for this was to wrap the affected member with strips of cloth soaked in salt solution – a somewhat painful cure which did eventually work.

A person suffering from happy feet and Changi balls was in a sorry state indeed, and there were many like that. Skin diseases were also prevalent; these were also treated with salt water, because there was not much else available.

In our quarters in Changi village life was tolerable even though vitamin deficiency persisted. Rations were reasonable – when supplemented by food grown by all ranks – and the other ranks were getting sufficient work shared amongst them to give them spending money. We were not unduly worried by our captors and life just went steadily on.

Sitting on our porch we thought of the couplet from Omar Khayyám, which we probably misquoted as:

a loaf of bread, a flask of wine, and thou
Would be paradise enow

We had rice instead of bread, alcohol had not been seen since we entered our POW life, and there was definitely no 'thou'.

Things, however, might have been different. Rumour had it that when we surrendered, Lieutenant General Percival went to meet the Japanese High Command to discuss the conditions under which we were going to live. After accommodation, food and pay had been settled, the Japanese said they were going to allow one comfort girl per ten officers. Percival's reply was 'Good God'.

The Japanese went into a huddle and came back and said that maybe they had been a bit stingy so how about one comfort girl per six officers.

Percival was stung to reply 'British officers do not need that kind of woman'. Back the Japanese went into another huddle and deliberated on the upbringing of British officers and their method of schooling and came back with an offer. They said it would be rather difficult, but they might manage one small boy per fifty officers. An enraged Percival retorted 'British officers do not do anything like that either'.

So the Japanese decided definitely that the British army had lost the campaign because the officers were all testicle handicapped. The story is almost certainly apocryphal, but there probably was a grain of truth in it. So there we were, doomed to lead a teetotal, monastic life. The Japanese informed us that we were now part of the South-East Asian Co-prosperity Sphere, called *Syonan-to*, and we now had to work for the prosperity of the region. Part of this included growing castor oil seeds to provide oil for the aeroplanes of the Japanese Air Force. Every person, officers and men, had to plant three seeds and tend them every day to ensure they grew.

Woe betide anybody if more than one seed died. In our Southern area we carefully planted our seeds, but we never saw them reach maturity because we moved when they were only half grown.

Besides castor oil plants, several vegetables were grown such as *kang kong*, a form of creeper with large green leaves, *bayam*, a Chinese vegetable resembling Chinese cabbage – but smaller and less compact – and Ceylon spinach, which had a red stem like thin rhubarb and dark green leaves. Ceylon spinach was very nutritious but contained a lot of oxalic acid which led to deposits of calcium oxalate under the skin; it was also not good for rheumatism.

Root vegetables to provide bulk included sweet potatoes, Chinese radish and tapioca plants. The latter grow like parsnips but the roots are much larger in size; after two years growth they can be up to two feet long. The tapioca of commerce is made by cutting up the root into small pieces called tapioca chips and drying them in the sun. The chips are then cut up and fried dry to make the small, round pellets of the tapioca bought in shops. This preparation is a skilled job and was highly paid in Malaya. Work parties tended the vegetable patch and that was one way for other ranks to earn pay.

Every morning there was *tenko*, roll call, to check the number of prisoners and also to form work parties for the day. One morning when the troops were feeling frisky, they numbered off as one, two, … nine, ten, jack, queen, king, ace. The Japanese officer said 'What is this ace?' We explained that the troops had had a momentary lapse of memory and that they were numbering in a way traditional in the Royal Artillery.

This saved the day as the artillery were very popular with the Japanese. We had caused 85 per cent of their casualties, so they thought we weren't too bad as soldiers. It may sound strange, in the light of present-day thinking, that the Japanese should applaud that branch of the army which had caused the greatest number of their casualties. Looked at in the light of professional armies fighting each other, honour was being given to a worthy opponent. Whether the casualty figures were correct or not, the fact remained that the Japanese were of the opinion that the artillery fought well, and were accordingly well disposed towards the gunners.

When the work parties were detailed, those working in Singapore went off in lorries for the whole day, accompanied by an officer from the battery.

The work in Singapore consisted of cleaning up the town and repairing roads, drains and buildings. There was a considerable amount of work to be done immediately after the surrender but by now, a year after, working parties had been reduced to a trickle. As the lorries drove into Singapore they passed several roundabouts. The Japanese used to display the heads of people executed by beheading, on planks on the roundabouts 'pour discourager les autres'. The troops used to sing a popular song of the time: 'I ain't got no body and nobody ain't got me'. The Japanese thought this was excruciatingly funny and laughed their heads off. The next popular song was 'A tisket a tasket a little yellow basket' – this reduced the Japanese to a state of fury.

In addition to gardening and clearing up there was a wood fatigue. Some of the captured British army vehicles had been stripped down to just a chassis with the steering wheel and a driver's seat. Pulled by a team of six to eight men using ropes these were used to collect wood. An officer went with the party, carrying a flag which said 'these are prisoners of war collecting wood'.

There were abandoned rubber estates within the overall perimeter of the camp, and the rubber trees were chopped down to provide wood for cooking fires. Rubber wood does not make a very good fuel but it was all that was available. No fires were needed to provide heating in the billets.

As there are no seasons in the tropics the temperature remains the same throughout the year, in Singapore averaging about 84°F during the day, and dropping by about four to six degrees at night. Clothing and heating are thus of no great importance.

Although our existence seemed pleasant enough, with no great worries except for a desire for more and interesting food, the difficulty was what to do throughout the day. This was fortunately solved by the existence of a good library. When the original working parties went to Singapore after the surrender, part of the town that had to be cleared up was in the university area, which had been part of the front line defence for the last week of the battle for the town.

The members of the working party managed to salvage masses of books and brought them back to camp. These were eventually organized in libraries, with full-time librarians looking after the books and organizing a proper lending system. It was possible to obtain books on any subject that a prisoner wished to study.

Amongst the prisoners were many people with an academic background, particularly the previous lecturers from Raffles College, an institution awarding tertiary academic qualifications. Such lecturers were in the Singapore Volunteer units; the professor of mathematics was a corporal in the machine-gun company of the Volunteers. A system of lectures was set up and anybody was free to attend classes that were on offer.

I had decided to study the Malay and Thai languages. Malay was an easy option in Southern area where all the Malay Volunteer Forces were billeted and teachers were offering lessons. Thai was a different matter. There was a European who had been a judge in Thailand and he offered a course but unfortunately the judge was in the Australian area, so I had to get to that area from Southern area.

There was a means of getting there provided by a bus service. This was not a vehicular service but consisted of an officer carrying a flag which stated in Japanese 'These are prisoners of war marching from one area to another'. The bus service ran to a timetable, posted up in all areas. At the bus stop, at the appointed time, the officer detailed for duty called the 'passengers' to fall in and then marched them off through the gate out of the area.

At the guardhouse, just outside the gate, the command 'eyes right' or 'eyes left' was given in Japanese, the commands being *'kashira hidari'* or *'kashira migi'* (phonetically spelt and maybe not exactly correct). The officer saluted the guard and the 'passengers' obeyed the command. The bus then marched along the road to the next area, saluted the guard and entered the area.

To get to my course I caught a bus to the hospital area and waited for the next bus to the Australian area. I attended my lecture at least twice a week, and the trip consumed an afternoon.

★   ★   ★

The layout of the various POW areas, linked by the existing road system, gave an opportunity for a black market to emerge. It began with prisoners trading items of their personal possessions for other items for which they had a greater need.

There was one story of an officer in another camp area – who had been an executive in Marks and Spencers before the war – starting with trading his sole possession of three razor blades. By working his way up, using successive trading ventures, he became well supplied with food and other useful items.

Eventually such activities extended beyond the camp areas into the surrounding countryside, as there were Chinese living inside the main perimeter wire, although not in the specific POW areas. These black market activities impinged on the regiment through one of its soldiers. There was a bombardier in the regiment who protested that, as an Irishman, he was a neutral subject and so should not be a prisoner. His claim for neutral-ity eventually found its way to the Japanese commandant, who agreed his status. The bombardier then departed – to the envy of all his comrades – to Singapore city. With his natural ability for blarney he set himself up with a Chinese girl and lived comfortably.

Like many regular soldiers, he was on the look-out for any opportunity to improve his life style, and this he found in the black market. By this time a thriving market had developed and, provided you had enough money, many luxuries were available, even a bottle of malt whisky. The bombardier became one of the operators on the Singapore side of this black economy, and flourished.

The Japanese guards were obviously unhappy that there was communication between POWs and the outside world, so the *Kernpei-tai* set about tracing the activities of the black marketeers. The bombardier was an obvious choice for investigation and in due course he was caught while engaged in his activities. He was brought back to Changi, and punished.

The punishment was to kneel on the tarmac in a courtyard in Changi Gaol, holding a log of wood above his head, with his arms stretched to their full height. This may not sound a severe punishment, but even after a few minutes the muscular strain becomes intolerable. A guard mounted over him did not allow him to relax the position in any way, and he spent from dawn to dusk in this position with no shade, and no water to drink, under a tropical sun. He was sent to the camp hospital in a state of collapse, and it was a considerable time before he was fit enough to return to the regiment.

★   ★   ★

Writing paper was in short supply and the copy of the *New York Times* was not of much use. Notes were taken on the paper from cigarette packets; the local cigarettes were sold in American style packets which, opened up, formed a small sheet of paper. The cigarette ration from the Japanese came from Red Cross parcels.

Someone with a warped sense of humour had put in the parcels cigarettes intended for Indian army troops and they had a large letter 'V' on the packet and were entitled 'V for victory'. Somehow they managed to get by the Japanese authorities and we received our ten cigarettes per week. This type of packet was also pressed into service, and additional empty packets obtained from people not using the paper for writing.

I also spent some time trying to improve my knowledge of Urdu, the *lingua franca* of the Indian army. This was on a one-to-one basis with a friend.

Urdu is an interesting language and was invented by Akbar, one of the Moghul emperors. He had officers who spoke Persian and soldiers who spoke Hindi, so he combined the two languages, with Persian supplying the abstract ideas and the higher class representative of an object and the Hindi supplying the lower class representative – the same as in English with Norman–French and Anglo Saxon. There were exact parallels for 'mansion' and 'house' in both languages.

Each Indian soldier spoke his own native language, such as Punjabi or Pushtu, and had to learn Urdu on joining the army. Ghurkas spoke their own language, together with Ghurkali, a *lingua franca* for Nepal, and also Urdu. Whilst fighting it is sometimes hard to remember the grammatical rules in a couple of other languages.

Thai, on the other hand, had the difficulty of being a tonal language where for instance the word '*na*' in five different tones can mean at least three different things, such as horse, aunt or field. You can have fun telling someone there are three aunts looking after five horses in two different fields. This causes no trouble to a Thai, but causes trouble to a European. The mental activity in studying these languages helped to keep one's mind alert.

The camp area was supplied with electricity, and probably our coolie quarters did have a supply. But it was not of much use as we had no light bulbs nor any electrical appliances. Once darkness fell it was difficult to follow any activity. Usually we sat around and just talked until bedtime. There was no 'lights out' – they were permanently out, so people went to bed when they felt like it, remembering there was roll call the next day and possibly a working party. At full moon it was light enough to play cards when sitting in the open, so bridge was popular with the officers, but this activity lasted for only a week at the outside and depended on there being no storm.

Generally it rains every day in Singapore, normally around four o'clock, with the evening being fine. There is no monsoon season in Malaya; the Malay name for the region is '*Tanah di bawah angin*' – the Land below the Winds. This produces a uniform climate throughout the year, which may appear monotonous but does have its advantages.

The other pastime was observing the stars. In the tropics the stars are much clearer and nearly always visible, so amateur astronomers gave brief lessons on star recognition. This also helped to pass the time during the evenings; the main object was trying to keep one's mind occupied. On those evenings when the moon provided no light, visits from friends brought news and discussions on all manner of topics.

The picture that emerges is of a boring – if peaceful – life. Boredom was the great enemy and gave rise to a feeling of frustration that life was passing you by and there were so many things you would like to be doing.

Being cooped up with the same people day in and day out also caused friction. A man's personal habits could cause irritation and there was no way of avoiding him when he was there all the time. This meant keeping a tight rein on your temper and trying to forget your fellow prisoner's irritating little habits. Occasionally tempers did flare up, but on the whole we all learnt to be much more tolerant and to choke back our feelings.

There was one episode that relieved the monotony. A soldier had been cut off from the regiment during the retreat down the Peninsular and he made his way down to Singapore. The Japanese captured him and as he had been on his own and they thought he had been spying, they sentenced him to execution.

He was brought down to the shore in Johore, opposite Singapore Island, at a beach where the Johore Straits are narrow. He was to be executed by beheading, but the officer carrying out the sentence was inexperienced and, instead of decapitation, wounded him on the shoulder. To the surprise of all, he jumped up, ran into the water, and swam over to Singapore Island, getting clean away.

He made his way to the camp and managed to get in. There, after having his wound dressed, he was shunted from unit to unit. Nobody wanted the responsibility of taking him on a unit strength so eventually he was delivered to the battery in Changi village, and became my responsibility.

The penalty for an incorrect roll call was severe, so he was hidden in our quarters during roll call, with a prayer that no wandering Japanese soldier, or the *Kempei-tai*, would find him.

Japanese guards occasionally wandered round the billets during roll call, with a possibility of finding the hidden soldier. The guards, however, were not the chief worry it was the *Kempei-tai* that were of greater concern. They usually operated in a group of three, mounted on bicycles, and rode round the various areas of the camp, looking into all aspects of camp life, both of the POWs and of the Japanese and Indian guards. Their punitive methods were probably responsible for most of the torture described by prisoners who experienced questioning and interrogation.

The most severe method of interrogation, used on very stubborn prisoners, was said to be the water treatment. A funnel was placed in the victim's mouth, and water slowly poured down the funnel. To escape drowning, the victim had to swallow the water continuously. Several pints of water were poured in, causing the victim's stomach to swell. The interrogator then hit the stomach, causing acute pain. Severe blows on the stomach caused rupture of the intestines, eventually resulting in a painful death.

This method of interrogation was certainly used on Chinese prisoners, but information on whether it was used on POWs did not reach the regiment while we were still in Changi.

For five days I went to successive padres, suggesting that the next time a man died, the escaped soldier should be given the dead man's name, but all refused because they said the idea was unethical.

I was not too happy with their ideas on ethics – both the escaped prisoner and I were under threat of execution. However, at last I did find a consenting padre, and the load was lifted from my shoulders. The escaped prisoner went into the hospital and after recovery lived through to the capitulation.

Meanwhile the war was dragging on and occasionally some real news would percolate through the camp. There were radios in the camp and news from the BBC was available but it was deemed better to keep good news in short supply so that the Japanese would not notice a feeling of elation amongst the prisoners.

Up to March 1943 there had not been much good news and everyone felt despondent, wondering whether we would ever get off the island. There was one ray of hope, perhaps. The Japanese High Command had stated that after ten years as prisoners we would have expiated our crime of confronting the Japanese Emperor in a belligerent manner. As a reward we would be given a Japanese wife, two acres and a cow, the idea being that we could provide replacements for the troops lost in battle. In the army vernacular the thought was expressed that the Japanese wife would provide the two 'achers' anyway.

The proposal did have some appeal – especially the Japanese wife – although we weren't too sure about the cow. Only another nine years to go and then we would be sampling the delights of rural Japanese bliss.

Many men had thought of escaping, as the Japanese guards were lax, but the nearest British forces were either in Australia or Burma. Australia was obviously a poor choice, unless a reliable boat was available, and even then there was a long sea journey through enemy-occupied areas.

Burma was a possibility, but it meant travelling 2,000 miles through countries where the inhabitants were overawed by the Japanese and could claim a reward for information concerning escaping prisoners. There were also about 500 miles of uninhabited jungle, mainly mountainous and definitely not neutral to people untrained in jungle survival. As rations were meagre saving them posed a problem and, in addition, rice and vegetables cannot be easily stored. On the whole, escape was almost impossible from Singapore.

All was about to change drastically and much for the worse.

# CHAPTER III

# The Orient Express to Ban Pong

Rumours were rife in the camp that the Japanese were building rest and recuperation camps in hill stations, although nobody knew where. No more parties were being sent abroad so everyone thought this could be true; the bulk of the remaining prisoners could best be described as convalescent. Various parties were detailed and left the camp, while we still lived on in Changi village, becoming more and more impatient because we thought we were missing out on this wonderful opportunity to go to a cool climate and just rest.

The Japanese word for rest is *yasmi* and these rumoured destinations were labelled in our imagination as Yasmi camps.

At last the word arrived and the battery had to provide about 50 other ranks and two officers, with myself detailed to be in charge. We were told to get together all the equipment that would be needed to keep everyone entertained in our new surroundings. We, as a battery, did not have much to offer, but other units supplied musical instruments, even pianos from the former army quarters, stage equipment for producing plays, and books for leisure and study.

Details of the organization filtered through the chain of command. We were to be organized into a battalion of 600 men, with a colonel in charge. So the sifting-out process began. I was a bit doubtful of the Japanese intentions, so selected only men that I thought might benefit from a sojourn in the hills, and ended up with 51 men, leaving behind those that were too sick.

I was to be in charge of a company of 100 then, with 49 men from the Volunteers, both Malaya and Singapore Volunteers, being included in my company. There were going to be six such companies and we were part of a formation called H Force. The six companies formed a battalion under the charge of the colonel, making a total of six hundred men. Later we found out that there were other battalions included in H Force.

Robert, the other officer with me in the company, was a gunner, and together we set about organizing the equipment we were going to take with us. It was not much; we had entered Changi bringing only what we could carry from Singapore. However, we had inherited sundry other objects from the previous parties that had left the camp for destinations overseas.

At last the day arrived for departure. Orders were issued to have a final meal in the evening and report to an assembly centre in Southern area. This we did and arrived early in the evening to meet with the detail of Volunteers who were to make up the company. They had considerably more baggage than we had, including a piano inherited from the army and naval quarters they had occupied in the area.

Lorries arrived, driven by Japanese soldiers, and we loaded all the equipment on to some of them. The company then embussed on the remaining lorries and we were ready for the first stage of our journey to the unknown rest and recuperation camps. We were all looking forward to our sojourn in a delightful hill station, with rest and recuperation the order of the day.

Each lorry took twenty-five men and their belongings. They were ordinary lorries with sides about three feet high and a tailboard which was fastened when all were aboard. There was room only to stand – and that not very comfortably because our kit was perched between our feet.

The Japanese drivers took off as though they were entering for the French Grand Prix and tore down the road to Singapore at a furious rate. When they came to a bend there was no slowing down and the lorry heeled over with the weight of the men. If you were on the outside you had to grab hold of your neighbour in order not to be thrown out; he in turn grabbed hold of his neighbour. The last man held on to the side like grim death to keep all aboard.

We eventually arrived at Singapore station, thoroughly exhausted by the transport experience, and disembussed. There we met the other companies and immediately started to unload. Rice trucks were waiting in the station and the equipment was off-loaded into some of them.

The Malayan railway has a metre guage so the rolling stock is smaller than the rolling stock in Britain. Each rice truck – so called because they were used for transporting rice – was about twenty-five feet long and seven feet wide and had two doors, one on each side, in the middle of the truck. These doors were about four feet or so wide. Across the door opening of the remainder of the trucks – those not being loaded with equipment – was a bamboo cane about an inch thick, fastened by wire to the truck. These trucks were for the transport of the POWs.

I reported to the colonel and was given the number of trucks to be used by the company. Four were allocated to us; two were loaded with twenty-five men and two with twenty-six men. Each truck had to contain men and their belongings so there was not overmuch room.

Rice trucks are made of steel – sides, roof and floor – not ideal for comfort, and the floor was certainly hard for sleeping on. We also soon found out that when the train moved off just after midnight the trucks could be distinctly chilly. The train travelled slowly up the line and, although Malayan trains were not noted for their speed because the guage limits the speed, this train seemed exceptionally slow. Even so, the motion set up a breeze through the trucks which cooled us down and then made us very cold.

The train passed over the Causeway joining Singapore Island to the mainland just before dawn broke and steamed up to a small station about eleven miles from the Causeway. Alongside the station were labourers' lines for men working on the railway. Most were Tamils from Southern India and, at this time of dawn, were performing their ablutions in the open outside their quarters.

When the train stopped all the prisoners alighted and were directed to food which had been prepared for us, the usual rice and vegetables. After we had eaten we received a cup of hot green tea. This had a disastrous effect – six hundred bowels moved as one. The low hills around the station were quickly populated with men squatting wherever they could, to the delight of the Tamil onlookers. The Japanese could do nothing about it and had to wait until all motions were brought to a satisfactory conclusion. They ran round the squatting men calling out '*bugeru, bugeru, oru men*' which on interpretation meant 'all men get a move on'. I never did find out what '*bugeru*' meant, but it definitely indicated a strong desire for attention to be paid to the next command. The other words were part of the Anglo-Japanese language that developed between guards and POWs.

The Japanese have difficulty in pronouncing the letter 'l' and substitute 'r' for it. This leads to such words as '*oiru*' for oil. The second difficulty of pronunciation is ending a word with a consonant, an impossibility for most people speaking an oriental language, unless the word ends in 'n', 'ng', or 'm' and a vowel has to be added after the final consonant. Hence *oiru* for oil and some quaint expressions such as 'I am frying on British Airways tonight'.

Everyone mounted their rice trucks with alacrity and the train steamed off at its usual leisurely pace. The sun was climbing higher in the sky and the walls of the trucks became steadily hotter and hotter. Inside we sweated and were soon stripped down to the waist in an effort to keep cool. The breeze from the train's motion was now welcome and as many as could stood by the open door, leaning on the bamboo cane.

After several hours a new use for the bamboo cane materialized. When bowels had to be opened, the solution was to sit on the cane, hold on to the truck wall with one hand and the bamboo cane with the other hand and hope to maintain a sense of balance. The rail track was used as a lavatory. Care had to be taken to use the leeward side of the truck when the wind was blowing.

The railway line in Malaya was a single track for most of the way and there were sidings at small stations and halts to allow other trains to pass. The driver was handed a large bamboo 'key' to show the single line was clear to the next siding. Our train had a low priority, so we waited at almost every siding for other trains to pass.

While waiting nobody was allowed to descend from the trucks. The guards travelled in coaches at each end of the train and were prepared to fire if any

POW actually got out of the train. This did not stop small boys and others from coming to the train and offering items of food on rush trays. We still had some money and we could purchase the odd item without the guards objecting, as long as we remained in the truck. Apart from such stops and an opportunity to buy something, we travelled without food or water from one meal to the next.

The ardours of the trip brought out underlying sickness in the men, but there was little that could be done to help them. They just had to lie on the floor of the truck and hope to recover. The main difficulty was thirst as the truck became hotter and hotter. Our stops were at infrequent intervals and the possibility of obtaining some form of liquid refreshment was slight; occasionally a green coconut containing coconut water could be bought.

The first scheduled stop was at a main station from which the local inhabitants had been excluded. Food was supplied as before and followed by warm green tea. The stay was short and we were bundled back on the train and off for another night. Thereafter, all our stops were at major stations with facilities for supplying food. At the end of the second day we stopped at Ipoh station, and this time the general public were not excluded. Apparently we were far enough away from headquarters at Singapore for the guard regime to relax. A crowd of hawkers was swarming around the station and extra food was available for anybody with money.

We had not had a wash since leaving our quarters in Singapore, so those men in trucks near the steam engine dashed up to the water supply for the engine and turned it on. At every major station there was a large tank with an arm that swung out, carrying a hose pipe about three inches across. This was used to top up the water supply of the engine. The men, stripped naked and enjoyed a shower. Obviously it was not possible for all six hundred to do likewise, so only a lucky few could avail themselves of the luxury. The guards did not seem to object.

The railway line from here on ascended hills towards Taiping and we had a change of scenery from rubber estates. We passed Taiping and descended to the northern plain of Malaya, an area with rice fields. The train drew in to Butterworth, a town on the mainland opposite Penang, where we had food and a prolonged wait. The main line on the Malayan railway system is in three sections, Singapore to Kuala Lumpur, Kuala Lumpur to Butterworth, and Butterworth to the Thai border. Our wait was to accommodate the change to the next section.

The train now passed through the state of Kedah with the countryside mainly composed of rice fields, which were empty at this time of year. Towards the end of the third day we arrived at the Thai border where our steam locomotive was exchanged for a Thai locomotive.

There was little difference in the terrain at this point, and indeed in the country generally, because we found the inhabitants of this part of Thailand spoke Malay as well as Thai. Unfortunately our Malayan money was now of no use, so no food could be purchased. The hawkers came to the train as usual and some bartering went on to exchange some personal items for food. An excellent bunch of small bananas could be bought for the equivalent of a few pence. These were called golden bananas and were excellent, being very sweet. In Malaya and Thailand there are different varieties of banana in the same way as there are different varieties of apples in Britain. Bananas can be used for savoury and dessert dishes. The countryside had now changed as we had moved out of tropical rain forest jungle into tropical monsoon forest. The trees were not so close together and the jungle was more open. There were definite seasons, with a dry season and a rainy season, the seasonal changes producing a different flora from the rain forest flora of Malaya.

The train speeded up and we travelled at a faster rate than in Malaya. This was just as well because food became much more infrequent. After five days on the train we arrived at Ban Pong, the junction for the Burma–Siam railway although we were not to know it at the time. We arrived at night and descended from the train, complete with our belongings.

After roll call and checking numbers the battalion was marched off a short distance to some huts which were long and about eighteen feet wide. The walls were made of woven palm leaves called *bertam*; this is a palm tree that grows in swamps and produces leaves that are quite stiff when dried and broad enough to be woven into a wall. The roof was made of *atap*, another type of palm tree with narrow leaves that are bent double round a bamboo cane which is about four feet long. Layers of these *ataps* are tied to rafters with an upper *atap* projecting over a lower one, to form a thatched roof, which provides good protection against heat and rain.

Along each wall was a low platform of bamboo called a *chang*. It was our first acquaintance with the ubiquitous bamboo. Bamboo belongs to the family of grasses and there are many different species; the ones used for the *changs* were about two inches in diameter. These bamboos are beaten flat and then beaten again to remove the nodes of the stems. The stems are marked with nodes about every six inches, depending on the size and species of bamboo. When flattened, the nodes stick up on the inside of the stem as sharp triangular pieces of woody material; these have to be removed by hammering.

The flattened bamboos were laid as a low platform, about six inches high, on either side of the hut, backing on to the wall. This left a passageway of about four feet, along which we walked to find a place on the *chang*. The whole company was tired, chilled and hungry; we just lay down on the *chang* and went to sleep.

Next morning we woke up and had to start the normal fatigues required in an army camp. The cooks went to a kitchen area and the troops carried the rations, rice and vegetables to the cookhouse. The morning meal was cooked and eaten, after which there was roll call for further duties.

The first of these duties was the unloading of our equipment from the rice trucks. This had to be manhandled from the sidings to huts in the camp – not a great distance, but carrying objects such as pianos took a long time. Our hearts sank to find the hut and other huts full of similar equipment. Obviously the equipment was not going to be used, in which case why had we laboured to bring it all the way from Singapore?

It began to look as if the idea of rest and recuperation was a myth. We certainly were not in a hilly district; Ban Pong is on the Thai coastal plain and the land around was as flat as a pancake. So the whole idea of rest and recuperation in a hill station had no reality. There were compensations. We had stand pipes providing water and were enabled to have a good wash and also wash our clothes which had become dirty on the railway trip.

The battalion stayed a couple of days at Ban Pong while the Japanese sorted out the next move. Then, after a morning meal, we fell in for a roll call and marched off carrying our belongings to a small town called Non Pladuk. This took the morning. There we were put into tents, obviously previously looted from the Indian Army. An Indian Army tent has an ordinary tent with an extra cover over the tent, giving two-layers between the occupants and the outside weather. This keeps out tropical rain and also the sun's heat. However, our tented accommodation consisted of either the tent or the covering, but not both.

Our cooking equipment had arrived and consisted of large *kualis*, or woks, about four feet in diameter. We had to make circular mounds of clay, baked hard, with an opening about one-quarter of the circle; the *kuali* was put on this mound and a fire lit underneath. This became the universal way of cooking for the whole of our period in Thailand. Rice was cooked in one *kuali* and stew in a second *kuali*. The stew was made of vegetables and, at Non Pladuk, a reasonable selection of vegetables was available.

On the morning of the next day we were paraded and marched off to a large bungalow, into which we were admitted as a slow stream of men. Inside were a selection of Japanese doctors waiting for us. In the first room our names were crossed off a battalion roll. In the second room an orderly grabbed your left arm, smeared alcohol on it and a doctor gave an injection.

The trail led through four rooms and in each room the same procedure was carried out on alternate arms, so we entered the sixth room with two injections in each arm. This room had a vaccinating team waiting for us and this time we were vaccinated against smallpox in the left arm which already had two injections in it.

The seventh room was prepared to give each man the order of the glass rod. We had had two of these glass rod episodes in Changi so we knew what was going to happen. On the order to bend, the trousers were lowered and the bare bottom presented to the doctor who proceeded to thrust a glass rod up the anus as far as he could. He then gave it a twirl and removed a specimen of faeces which was deposited on a Petri dish for examination.

The test was to determine whether anyone was suffering from an intestinal disease. As we never heard of any result, we presumed it was a face-saving exercise to show proper medical care was being carried out. We were told that the injections were for TAB, tetanus, cholera, and typhus, so by now we were supposed to be resistant to most diseases.

Our first experience of the glass rod in Changi had produced some amusing sights. One young recruit in the regiment, on receiving the glass rod, let out a roar like an enraged bull, took off at a smart speed and was seen running round the parade ground with the glass rod sticking out behind him. He was caught and duly admonished.

One of the subalterns in the regiment was very plump and the Japanese technician had some difficulty in finding his anus amongst the rolls of fat. The C.O. quickly summed up the situation and called out in his best parade ground voice 'Mr Smith pull the cheeks of the arse firmly apart'; entry was duly effected.

The battalion staggered out of the bungalow at Non Pladuk with everyone feeling sore in both arms, and the rest of the day was passed with no further fatigues or work. On the next morning the normal duties were resumed and parties detailed for the various odd jobs needed for the camp to function properly. This was no easy task for men whose arms had become red and swollen. In addition there were the members of my company from the Volunteers who were not fit for work anyway.

When the Volunteers had chosen their complement for the H Force, they had believed the Japanese and had selected people who were definitely convalescent. The oldest member of my company was in his middle fifties, and had been a senior bank manager with the Chartered Bank; he was not fit even to march and carry his belongings. So when I received details of the fatigue parties the company had to provide, I attempted to shelter such people by giving them the lightest possible tasks – preferably none at all. This did impose a strain on the other members of the company, but all could see the necessity and there was little grumbling.

Here we received our first pay in ticals, the currency of Thailand. Thai money nowadays is quoted in baht, but baht is the numerical coefficient for square objects. A numerical coefficient is the word used to describe a number of objects, as in English with 'three head of cattle', the word 'head' is used as a numerical coefficient. In Thai all objects have specific numerical coefficients as nouns do not have plural forms, so numbers have to be stated using the required numerical coefficients.

I received a month's pay and, as we were no longer in Changi, I received the full amount of 30 ticals. The men were paid for the work they had done and so we all had some pay.

The battalion was allowed a further day in which to rest and recover from the inoculations. During this time the camp fatigues were carried out, while our arms became a little less painful. Clothes were washed and dried and we were becoming prepared for our march up country, which the Japanese had told us was where we were going.

# CHAPTER IV

# The long march

The camp was woken up while it was still dark and we ate a breakfast of rice and vegetables in the dark. Parade was held and roll call taken with the company in its marching order. As dawn appeared, the battalion was marched off up the road out of Non Pladuk.

The countryside was flat and the dirt road was dusty because this was the dry season. Our belongings did not make marching easy. I had a pack on my back and carried my four-gallon petrol tin in one hand; this contained sundry useful odds and ends, such as a cup, plates and eating utensils.

We were not long on our way before the first people began to feel the strain of marching under tropical conditions. The cool of the morning was beginning to go and the heat of the day take over.

There were about twenty Japanese guards marching with us, some in the lead, and a larger contingent bringing up the rear to coerce the stragglers to keep up with the party. A halt was called and we rested for ten minutes or so, giving time for the stragglers to catch up, and then we were off again.

The older men in my company began to fall to the rear. We tried to help them with their belongings, but the guards kept pushing the main body forward. After the second or third rest period, people began to throw away the heavier items of their belongings, having decided what was worth keeping and what was not.

Some had water bottles, which they had filled in Non Pladuk, and water became essential as we toiled through the day. The heat and the dust from the road created a thirst. No water was available on the route and we marched from dawn until mid-afternoon.

The day's march ended at a Thai school, where we were told we would rest for the night. The school was by a river, and everybody rushed down to the river to bathe – most important of all to bathe one's feet. At least half the battalion had blisters. Having been POWs for over a year, our footwear was in poor condition and many men did not have socks. The sweating caused by marching soon raised blisters under these conditions.

There was nothing to be done to treat the blisters. We had no first aid equipment and the Japanese supplied none. Bathing helped soothe the sore foot, but did not relieve the condition. No transport was available for the sick.

The Japanese provided food at the school and this we ate just before it became dusk. By this time the stragglers had arrived; they were fed as well and the battalion then settled down for the night.

The Thai school was scrupulously clean and the buildings were well kept. We had the use of the buildings and some lay down to sleep on the floors. For those who could appreciate it the setting was delightful, well kept surroundings and a charming building which seemed to us like paradise after Non Pladuk.

There was not enough room to accommodate all the battalion, and most of them slept outside. The night was warm and being out in the open was very pleasant, all being grateful for the respite from marching.

The next day was a repeat performance except that there were more stragglers, with the guards becoming angry at the number falling behind. Once again, in the mid-afternoon, we arrived at the outskirts of a small town. We were shepherded into a compound with wooden buildings; this time there was no river nearby.

Some water was available from taps and bathing was carried out with difficulty. We were fed as usual and again slept out in the open. The following morning we departed at dawn and very soon came to a long wooden bridge, built on a cantilever principle.

We crossed the bridge, not knowing at that time that it was to become one of the most famous bridges in the world. It was the bridge over the River Kwai.

Once across the Kwai, the country became hillier and the road started to climb gently. It was still hot and dusty and now, in addition, we were climbing and not walking, along a flat road. This made marching more difficult, and the stragglers became more numerous. Even the guards were beginning to feel the strain and some of them were straggling too.

By the end of the day a few of the guards were getting POWs to carry their equipment, as they too were footsore and weary. All semblance of an organized march had disappeared, and everybody was just grimly struggling on, determined not to drop out.

And so we reached a small wayside halt where there was a repair station for railway rolling stock. I was roughly in the middle of the marching battalion, which was now so extended that both the front and the rear were well out of sight. Two ragged British soldiers ran from the repair station towards us; there were no guards in sight. They said we were the first British troops they had seen for a long time and asked where we had come from and where we were going. We could tell them we had come from Singapore, but had no idea where we were going. Their next question caused consternation – they asked us what year it was. We said it was about March 1943, and they said 'Good God, we've only been here six months; it has seemed like years'. They were engineers and had been detached from their original company to help the Japanese maintain their trucks.

They departed before the guards could see them. They were not guarded, just working with Japanese engineers. This conversation did not cheer us up; we realized that we would experience the same conditions where continuous work destroyed a sense of time.

We camped again at a small settlement and were fed. Next morning the march resumed; by this time all the troops and guards were weary. The whole battalion was stretched out over quite a distance. In the late afternoon we straggled into a major camp and thankfully sat down to rest. Stragglers kept arriving well into the night. Food was only provided for those who had arrived on time.

We learnt we had reached a base camp called Tarsao and had marched about 90 miles in four days. Considering we were supposed to be convalescent troops this was not a bad feat. At Tarsao, we met some other British troops we had known in Changi. They had come up on earlier working parties and were now old hands at living under the conditions of building a railway. Tarsao camp was carved out of the jungle and was full of large trees still standing, while the undergrowth had been cleared to make the camp. We were not given any accommodation, so just lay down on the ground where we were put by the guards.

When night fell the jungle awoke and the noise of insects was very loud. We thought there was a saw mill operating in the neighbourhood; the noise was almost deafening. However, it turned out to be the love call of the cicadas, insect-like grasshoppers but much larger and much noisier.

The Japanese soldiers would catch cicadas, hold them tightly in their hand, and then release the hand slightly, so that the cicadas could produce their rasping sound. In this way they could send Morse code over quite long distances.

The battalion had two days rest at Tarsao, allowing both troops and guards to recover from their march up country. There were no confined spaces; the camp was one large clearing in the jungle and as long as roll call was attended we could walk where we wanted.

Moving around I met friends from Changi and one evening a friend whom I had last seen in England two years ago. One other delight was the presence of Thai and Chinese eating stalls. There we could buy a Bah Mee served in a bowl, a pleasant change from eating the inevitable rice and vegetables.

A Bah Mee would not be recognised in a Chinese restaurant in England. The cook took a prawn, smashed it flat with a chopper, added an onion or two, and fried them together in a wok, using coconut oil. The onions and prawn were then removed and a few pieces of pork fried in the oil, flavoured by the onions and prawn. To the frying meat was added some flat Hokien noodles, and then the onions and prawn were put back in and some green vegetables added. Frying was stopped, water added and the whole boiled for a minute or two. The result was delicious, the taste of the pork making us quite ecstatic.

All our stragglers had arrived and we managed to get some dressings for their sore feet, as the working parties in Tarsao had a medical group looking after them. While we were happy to be resting there, the place itself filled us with gloom.

We were now in monsoon tropical jungle and though it was not as thick as tropical rainforest jungle, the tall trees gave it an eerie appearance. Lianas hung from the trees and the sunlight was greatly reduced in the shade – it was not unlike a dim cathedral.

After our two-day respite we fell in and were marched off at dawn, following a dirt road which climbed steadily uphill away from Tarsao. We were now entering the foothills which led to the mountainous interior region of Thailand. Almost immediately troops began to straggle but were shepherded along by the guards with shouts of '*Kura kura bugero*', which roughly translated means 'get a move on, you lazy so and so'. Slow walkers were encouraged with a rifle butt as speed seemed to be required. Later we saw the reason for this speed.

We marched for about six kilometres and then suddenly in the middle of nowhere on the dirt road through the jungle, the guards said 'Camp'. We asked 'Where'. The answer was 'Here'.

We were nonplussed, but lorries arrived carrying tools and kitchen equipment, so we realized we had to make a camp in the jungle there and then. Hence the speed; the guards also wanted a camp made for them before night fell.

The lorries delivered machetes, *changkols*, Assam forks, and root extractors. *Changkols* are spades attached at right angles to a haft; Assam forks are forks similarly attached at right angles to a haft. The British army in the First World War used an entrenching tool which was shaped like a *changkol*. They are excellent tools for digging up earth and were always in use on the railway.

The battalion was organized into parties to fell the trees, bamboos and other growth, to move the felled wood, remove the tree stumps, and flatten the earth. The first space cleared was for the cookhouse so that a midday meal could be provided; after that a general space was cleared to form the camp area.

All ranks took part in the clearing operation and a space rapidly appeared in the jungle. We were higher than the coastal plain; the jungle was much less dense and mainly characterized by a lot of bamboo.

Bamboo grows in clumps with different varieties having different girths and different heights. All had shoots growing at the base of the clump and these took a lot of excavation to get the ground clear. There are male and female bamboos, with the female having a hollow stem and the male having a solid stem; the diameter of a male stem is less than that of a female stem. In the clump female bamboos vastly outnumbered male bamboos.

Bamboos flower very rarely – only once in every thirty to forty years – and when they do the whole vegetation dies and a new generation grows up in place of the former generation. Such facts took time to find out, but we gradually learnt as we came to use bamboo more and more in all our work.

As we cleared the ground, tree trunks, branches and tall bamboos fell against us; the work force was closely packed to achieve maximum clearance. We did not know then how dangerous growing bamboo was. Only later did we learn that a cut caused by a bamboo stem almost always turned into a tropical ulcer.

I was working next to a member of the Volunteer force and as we were cutting down a large clump of bamboo a tall stem fell across our legs. We took no notice of it and went on working.

That night I bathed my leg as it felt itchy, but I think my co-worker did not. I developed a scratch which was red, but after bathing it every night it vanished to leave three white scars which I had for the rest of my time in Thailand. The Volunteer developed an ulcer and was eventually shipped off to a base camp for sick people. There he lost his leg; it had to be amputated because the ulcer would not heal.

After working all day cutting down the jungle, sufficient space was cleared to erect tents that had been supplied by the Japanese and, having had a meal, we lay down glad of a rest. The next morning we were up before sunrise, fed, and started work again enlarging the clearing. This went on for about three days, by which time we had enough space for a tented camp for the POWs and a separate space for the guards.

The officers were provided with a square Indian Army bell tent, as usual without the outside cover. In this tent twenty officers and their baggage were crammed; some had a fair amount of baggage, but most did not have much. The colonel and the adjutant of the battalion had a separate tent, while the other ranks were crowded into Indian Army tents – either a tent or its cover.

No bedding was supplied, so we lay on the ground, using what material we had against the damp. I had an old gas cape which served as a ground sheet, and I used my pack as a pillow. After eating our food we retired to bed too tired to do anything else, wearing our everyday clothes as we had nothing to change into. Food was eaten squatting on our belongings.

On about the third or fourth night we were lying on our piece of ground, and I was trying to get to sleep but finding it difficult. Suddenly I heard a quiet, querulous whisper from one of the occupants lying two officers away from me. He said 'Is anyone awake?' The following conversation then took place in whispers, with me answering the plaintive call. 'Yes Jones I am awake, what's the matter?' 'There's a snake up my trouser leg.' 'Where is the snake's head?' 'Too bloody close.' 'OK, I'll wake the rest quietly and we'll see what we can do.'

I woke up the others as quietly as possible and got everybody outside the tent, where we discussed what could be done. Obviously the snake had to be treated very delicately; we did not know what kind of snake it was and whether it was poisonous or not.

One of the doctors had lived in South Africa and he said he had watched natives deal with snakes they had found hiding in crannies in walls. They grasped the snake by the tail, quickly pulled it out and cracked it like a whip, breaking its back. We decided this was the only possible solution and the doctor said he was willing to try. If he did not succeed the snake would bite him, and possibly Jones as well.

We went into the tent as quietly as possible and cleared a path from Jones' leg to the tent opening. Luckily he was almost opposite the entrance, which made the task a little easier. Our only candle – all of two inches long – was lit and held carefully near the snake's tail, taking care not to spill any hot candle wax on the snake.

The doctor dried his hands to get a good grip on the snake and we went outside, in line with the entrance, with sticks in our hands. The doctor took a deep breath, gripped the snake's tail, pulled hard, cracked it like a whip and threw it outside to the waiting men. We hit it with our sticks and killed it, although the doctor had broken its back and it was powerless to do any harm. When we were convinced it was dead we went to see how Jones was faring. He had fainted.

We settled down for the night, but it was impossible to get to sleep thinking of that snake and how it must have clambered over about half a dozen people to get to Jones at the back of the tent.

The next morning we took the snake to the Volunteers for identification. It was a nasty looking specimen, coloured yellow, purple and black, with a large head and a long body. It was identified as a bamboo snake, one that lived in bamboo clumps, and very poisonous. We were dismayed to find that they lived in pairs and that its mate would come looking for it.

The officer living next to the entrance was an Australian who had a better collection of belongings than the rest of us. Luckily it included a torch, although he was worried that the battery was getting near its end. We equipped ourselves with sticks and the next two nights tried to sleep without thinking of the snake's mate.

On the third night the Australian officer woke up in the middle of the night and said 'It's here'. Most of us were awake and those not near the snake rose silently, while the Australian shone the torch on the snake, which was making straight for me. The other occupants leapt over the baggage and hit the snake with their sticks, killing it.

We all felt much relieved and managed to get to sleep without further worry. The episode had not endeared us to sleeping on the ground, but there was nothing to be done about it. We were now having to take working parties out every day and were too busy to improve the amenities in the tent.

The working parties on the railway had indeed begun in earnest. We marched out as a battalion and started to clear a road down to the place where the railway would run. Japanese engineers had marked out the line of the track and we began to clear the jungle along the proposed line.

In the meantime we were still enlarging the camp to provide enough space for all the requirements of an army camp. This was done by parties mainly recruited from the sick, labelled as 'medicine and duty', to save them the extra labour of marching to work.

The cookhouse area was expanded to contain the rations which were arriving by lorry. We also built a hospital area; by this time we had quite a few patients admitted to hospital, particularly the older members of my company. General medical care was carried out by our own doctors, who also took care of the patients in hospital.

The guards required a special area to be cleared for them and then proceeded to set up a few home comforts. One we envied most was two or three large oil drums, each about five feet high and of corresponding diameter. These were filled with hot water, and the Japanese troops used to luxuriate in a hot bath. It was then we learnt the value of a water supply.

The guard area was separate from our area and the guards used tents similar to ours, but obviously of better construction. They had their own cookhouse and cooks were seconded from the battalion to look after them. We still did not know much about the guards; we were too busy trying to establish ourselves with such little luxuries as we could manage.

For the hospital area we managed to get ridge tents, and in these we constructed our first *changs*, made of flattened bamboo. They were held together on a bamboo framework by thin strips of bamboo and had bamboo legs for support. This arrangement kept the sick off the ground and gave them a fighting chance of survival. Each hospital tent had two *changs* running down the side of the tent, and the patients slept on them, with a British medical officer carrying out inspections.

The number working on the camp was slowly being reduced and the majority of the men went out to work on the railway. The camp was eventually finished; barbed wire was supplied and the POW area was ringed round with it. We were not sure whether the barbed wire was to keep us in, or other people out.

At roll call in the morning the various tasks were given out by the Japanese and if you were working outside you moved off at dawn. I was usually detailed with my company to work on the railway route. My numbers were by now seriously depleted as the older Volunteer members were falling sick at an alarming rate. My gunners were also beginning to get sick.

The initial work, clearing the route to be followed by the railway, involved cutting down trees, removing them and the undergrowth and making a clear passage about thirty to forty feet wide. Each day a little more was cleared and the route extended. Eventually we would join up with the work being done by groups on either side of us.

We were isolated from all other camps to begin with, but gradually the picture was filled in as we learnt about the other groups working on the railway. Our camp was called Tonchan South and we were part of a group in the Tonchan area involving three camps, called Tonchan North, Tonchan, and Tonchan South. The River Kwai flows roughly north-south and the road and railway route ran almost parallel to the river, so we were the most southerly camp of the group.

The camp had no readily available source of overseas news and was dependent on odd scraps of information leaking through the camps. We did have a radio – belonging to the Australian officer in the officers' tent – cunningly concealed in a Dutch water bottle.

The Dutch water bottles were larger than their British equivalent and were circular in shape, like a thick slice of sausage, with a corked neck. The top half of the bottle was covered in cloth and the bottom half was metal. The radio was in the lower half and sealed in so that water could be put in the top half. When examined by any guard, water could convincingly be poured out of the bottle.

Unfortunately there were no charged batteries to work the radio, and we had to wait for an opportunity to get hold of suitable batteries from anyone passing. Much later on we obtained some, but for the present we lived in a state of ignorance of the outside world.

Thus we began our work of railway construction.

# CHAPTER V

# Heigh-ho, heigh-ho, and off to work we go

The camp at Tonchan South was organized as a military formation. The battalion of POWs consisted of six companies each of one hundred men under the charge of two officers. The commanding officer was a lieutenant-Colonel and the headquarters staff consisted of an adjutant, a captain, and a quartermaster, a lieutenant.

Three British doctors provided medical attention; they had come from either British or Indian army formations. The battalion had two padres – one Anglican and one Catholic – as the Japanese were sympathetic to religious observances. In addition we had an interpreter, a former English missionary who spoke fluent Japanese and an accountant, a British army officer, to keep track of the wages earned by the troops when working.

A contingent of Japanese engineers was in charge of our section of the railway and we built huts next to, but not part of, the camp, for their accommodation. The guards were in the same compound as the engineers, and all the Japanese personnel were living with some degree of comfort compared with the POWs.

The Japanese engineers decided what work would be carried out each day and how many men they thought were necessary to perform the tasks. This quota of men was then the subject of an argument between the colonel and adjutant and the Japanese. The work parties had to be balanced against the number of men required for camp fatigues to maintain the camp and also the number of sick, both those hospitalized and those fit for medicine and duty.

Having decided the tasks, and the quota of men for each task, the parties were detailed on the morning roll call. Tools and other implements required for all duties were issued by the quartermaster who was in charge of equipment. The tools were given out at roll call and the various working parties moved off to carry out their work under the charge of guards, leaving one or two guards in the camp.

The accountant moved from camp to camp to maintain the pay records and, in doing so, brought us news of other camps and occasionally outside news as well. The padres assisted in caring for those in hospital; the Japanese tried to keep down the numbers in hospital because their absence from work slowed down the process of building the railway.

The names of the camps still cause some difficulty. First of all there was usually a Thai name for a particular location but the English alphabet did not cope very successfully with transliteration of the Thai alphabet. This name was anglicised by the British, and further corrupted by the troops into something more recognizable in English. The Thai name of Kong Kuita became Konkoita and finally 'concreeta'. The Japanese further muddled the situation by using Japanese pronunciation, such as Wang Lan becoming Wanran.

To understand the tasks involved in constructing the railway a knowledge of the terrain is required. The land was hilly and as it sloped down to the River Kwai the hills were interspersed with gullies. Some of the gullies were small, others were deep and wide.

At this time of the year, in the dry season, all the gullies were dry but when the monsoon rains came they would have swiftly flowing water. It was thus not possible to fill them with earth; instead small bridges had to be built across each gully.

In between gullies the land could rise to quite a height. The railway path through the jungle had to be levelled by digging away the little hillocks, filling in down to the gullies and then bridging them. To achieve a level track a lot of earth had to be moved.

The tools used for shifting earth were the Assam forks, *changkols* and *pungkis*. A *pungkis* is a basket shaped like a shovel, made of woven rattan, with a handle on each side. In size it was about one foot wide and one foot long, so when heaped with earth, it could hold a considerable weight and required two men to carry it.

The Assam forks loosened any hard soil, the *changkols* dug the soil up and it was then loaded on to a *pungkis* to be carried to the area where it was needed. After the ground was levelled a small embankment was made on which the railway lines were to be laid. Drains at the side of the embankment allowed rain to run off the railway track to prevent it becoming waterlogged.

The engineers directed the officers of a company and the officers directed the men; there was a certain language difficulty in getting clear instructions. The Japanese wanted maximum work out of the men, whereas the men wanted to do as little as possible. In some cases they were not fit to do much more than the barest minimum, owing to subclinical diseases.

The officers were thus in the middle of the argument and it needed very careful thought to maintain a balance between the demands of the Japanese and the reluctance of the men. Were you to get a reputation as a 'Nip lover' or a 'men defender'? This could vary with the work to be done, the mood of the Japanese, the mood of the men, and the weather.

To go one stage up, the colonel had the difficulty of arguing with the Japanese to determine the number of men who were sick and definitely unfit for duty. This limited the remaining number available for work. It made the tasks of the working parties harder as the engineers were working to a strict program irrespective of the number of men engaged on a task. Those officers who acquiesced too much with Japanese demands were castigated as 'white nips'. Those who held out against Japanese demands were considered good commanders. Either way it was not an easy life to lead.

As for the Japanese, the engineers were expected to keep up with their schedules, and senior officers came round on inspections to see the progress made. If the schedule was falling behind the engineers were reprimanded. They in turn reprimanded the guards, who then attacked the POW officers. So from Japanese officers to working troops there was a distinct line of reprimand which grew more severe the lower down the line it went.

The railway line became a succession of cuttings and bridges to maintain a uniform gradient for the track. Bridges over small gullies were simple affairs: two vertical posts were driven into the earth and a cross-piece nailed to the uprights to make a simple support. This technique was used for most bridges. They needed many posts to form the supports, so one working party would cut down trees which were then sawn up to make suitable posts for both uprights and cross-pieces. To begin with, the provision of tree trunks was carried out by the working parties, but this organization was subsequently altered.

The tree felling parties were equipped with cross-cut saws and axes. After the trees had been felled they were collected by elephants and dragged off to a saw mill. At Tonchan South we never saw the saw mills and did not even hear them, but later on I was to come into contact with them.

The elephants were truly amazing. The driver, a *mahout*, would take the elephant up to a log and, using its tusks, the elephant would manoeuvre the tree into a suitable position for it to be tied with chains. These were attached to the elephant, who would then haul the tree off to a collecting point.

Dead on four o'clock the elephants would stop whatever they were doing and would be taken off to their camp. Most of us no longer had a watch, but those who did said the elephants were never more than a minute out – and that was without an elephants' union. Nobody knew where the animals were kept; they must have had a camp somewhere, but our information service was restricted to other POW camps. The elephants appeared at the start of the day and disappeared at the end of the day. We, as POWs, were isolated from the rest of the Japanese organization building the railway.

About this time the Japanese engineers had a bright idea to save themselves work. Each day a schedule had been imposed on them and they knew how far each stage of the railway should progress. To save the trouble of a daily measuring of progress, they devised the idea of issuing bamboo rods, each one metre in length. The rods were given to each working party and at the end of the day's labours they were placed against the work done. Sufficient rods were issued at roll call for the tasks of the day so that the engineers could measure the actual progress. But the troops – with the usual cunning of the underprivileged – cut off a few millimetres from each rod each day.

Placed against the day's work, a satisfactory result was obtained. This went on for about a week and then the engineers made a correct survey. To their horror, they were behind schedule – but how had it happened? It took them some time to actually remeasure the rods and then they found they had been cheated by a couple of centimetres on each rod. The troops had been very careful to keep all rods of the same length so that individual differences would not show up when they were checked.

When the reason for the discrepancies was finally solved, there was great trouble. The engineers slapped the faces of guards and officers, and the guards continued the exercise with interest. Needless to say, the troops responsible for the action got clear away.

The rations supplied by the Japanese had not varied from the time we arrived at Tonchan South. There was a generous allowance of rice, nearly one pound per man per day for those on working parties. This enabled us to feed the sick in hospital, who received no rations. Here again the colonel had to make a fine distinction between workers and sick so that everyone could have a reasonable ration of food.

For vegetables we received dried seaweed and nothing else. The Japanese said this was very nutritious but it was hard to believe them. It looked like green plastic and had roughly the same consistency; even when boiled it was distinctly chewy and took some time to masticate.

The troops, with their inimitable sense of apt description, labelled it 'gas cape stew'. For those who knew the gas capes issued to the army in the Second World War, it was a marvellous description. The seaweed was utterly tasteless and difficult to digest. Pieces of it floated in a thin watery stew. To give some taste to the stew we were issued with dried fish. Although dried, it had a slimy consistency and looked like a piece of wet haddock, complete with skin. A little more drying and it would have made excellent Bombay duck, as used with curry in the better Indian restaurants. It was also full of bones and these had to be carefully extracted when chewing the fish – not that we received all that amount in a ration of stew.

There were thus two ingredients of the stew, gas cape seaweed and fish, and the final watery product was served with plain boiled white rice, at both lunch or dinner if you were in camp. If you were on a working party a little stew and a lot of rice was brought out to the working party. The meal was revolting, but being hungry we ate it. The cooks made porridge for breakfast, which was rice cooked with more than the usual amount of water – a dish the Javanese called pap. To provide some interest in the food, the cooks tried toasting the rice until it was brown. This brown rice would then be made into porridge as well as the white rice, so you had a choice on the menu of white or toasted rice pap.

The fish supplied as described was called Number 2 fish. There was a Number 1 fish which was slightly more like a recognizable piece of fish. It was also sun cured, like the Number 2 fish, but had a rather nice cheesy flavour on top of the fishy taste, rather like *sole au gratin*. Cooked by itself this was reasonably pleasant to eat, but put in a stew was not so good. A lot of POWs were turned against fish, especially fish stews, for the rest of their lives.

To wash down these detectable meals, we were issued with green tea. The tea leaves were boiled with the water and it did make a refreshing drink.

After some time on this dreary diet we complained to the Japanese that the food was tasteless. 'Ah so' they said, 'we will see what we can do for you'. The result was an issue of pepper – one ounce per man per day. This is rather a lot of pepper but it went into the stew, making a strange combination that was excessively chilli hot to the taste buds. The cooks were informed about this and cut down the amount put in the stew.

The Japanese saw the mound of pepper growing each day and took objection to it. They said 'You wanted taste in your food. We supplied taste. Now you are refusing to eat the tasty stew. In future all the pepper will be used in the stew'. The cooks managed to burn some of it, but on the whole we had very 'tasty' stew – and developed quite a resistance to peppery food.

For reasons of simplicity, the Japanese army, wherever stationed, kept Tokyo time. Tokyo time was one and a half hours ahead of Thai time, so the Japanese woke the battalion at 4.30 in the morning, when it was still night. Sunrise was at six o'clock Thai time but 7.30 Tokyo time. On the other hand, instead of finishing work at six o'clock in the evening, we finished at 4.30pm. This allowed an hour and a half of daylight for eating a meal and cleaning up after the day's work.

When the battalion arrived at Tonchan South, our Japanese guards were exchanged for Korean guards. This was a change for the worse, since the Japanese tended to despise Koreans as a subject race; there was a further language barrier because the Koreans spoke their own language and Japanese was a foreign language to them.

The Japanese were harsh to the Korean guards and the guards vented their displeasure on the POWs. Our Korean guards were given the nicknames of Snow White and the seven dwarfs. Each 'dwarf' was given an appropriate name and there were recognizable versions of Dopey, Grumpy, Doc, Sleepy, etc. – only these guards were not fairies.

The Korean guards were always getting into trouble for slackness and the Japanese would line them up and have a ceremonial face-slapping to improve discipline. This treatment rebounded on us. The loss of face by the Koreans, because of the slapping in front of the POWs, tempted them to slap the faces of POWs on the slightest pretext.

One of the usual causes of disagreement with the guards was over the number of troops reporting sick. On one occasion the guards lined up the doctors and indulged in a prolonged session of face-slapping, particularly focused on one doctor who refused to reduce the number he had listed as unfit for any duty. The sick were made to parade to ensure they were genuinely ill. This delayed roll call and the engineers then became annoyed, so bad tempers ensued for the remainder of the day. The general opinion was that Korean guards were far harsher than Japanese guards.

Later on we found that other camps had Taiwanese guards and reports said these were much more sadistic than even the Korean guards. Our guards could obviously have been worse. Their response to different situations was puzzling to our Western minds, and some of their reactions we found very odd.

A story had come down to us from one of the camps to the north, at a place called Hin Tok. This was the location of a huge cutting and was considered to be one of the worst camps on the railway. Two British soldiers there, one a tall brawny Scot, and the other a small Londoner, were inseparable friends. One day as they were working at digging the cutting, the Londoner annoyed one of the guards, who shouted at him to work harder. The Londoner replied with a rude gesture, whereupon the guard lifted up his rifle and killed him with a single blow. The Scot was incensed with this action, so he picked up a stone and threw it at the guard, killing him.

Everybody held their breath as this seemed a recipe for disaster, but to the surprise of all, the Japanese just laughed and said 'What a clot, a no-good Japanese soldier, he should have got out of the way'. An action such as this appears incredible to Western thought, and there were other similar, but less serious, incidents that amazed us at the time.

At a later stage in my stay in Thailand, we discussed with a Japanese NCO the Japanese method of disciplining soldiers by face-slapping. He pointed out that it was used for minor disciplinary actions. A verbal reprimand was the first step, followed by a face slap, and then a slap in the presence of other soldiers, including junior ranks.

The presence of other soldiers made the offender lose face, a serious occurrence for an Asian. The officers slapped the faces of NCOs and men, the NCOs slapped the faces of men, and all slapped the faces of POWs.

As the Japanese NCO with whom we discussed this method of maintaining discipline said, the effect was quicker, consumed less paper and was most suitable to wartime conditions. It was mainly employed when an order had been carried out in a slapdash way or even ignored. More serious crimes were dealt with by methods akin to courts-martial in the British army.

To put this method of maintaining discipline in perspective, the social gradations of Japanese society are more marked and of greater difference than any corresponding gradations in Western society. Higher levels of society look on lower levels with contempt, and lower levels offer deference to higher levels; the greater the difference in social standing the greater the reaction. This is reflected in the language with abrupt forms and obsequious forms of a verb.

Tropical diseases were now starting to take their toll on the battalion. Malaria became common, although we could not distinguish between the benign and the malignant forms as we had no means of carrying out a microscopical examination of blood.

Other fevers also appeared, which in Singapore were labelled as NYD – not yet discovered. The Japanese provided quinine for the treatment of malaria, and this was used for other fevers just in case they might be malaria.

The diet was causing stomach upsets and eventually dysentery appeared in the camp, both bacillary and amoebic forms. For all intestinal complaints the Japanese provided little black pills of charcoal, but it was problematical whether the pills provided any relief, let alone cure.

For bacillary dysentery, the most prevalent form, a dose of Epson salts was given in an attempt to flush the bacteria out of the system. This, followed by a little starvation, effected some form of cure. With the unsatisfactory diet available, recovery was not easy because the food irritated the bowels.

Amoebic dysentery was harder to cure. There was a small supply of emetin occasionally available, otherwise only the little black charcoal pills were administered. A person could suffer from amoebic dysentery for some time without it becoming crippling, and many suffered permanently from it. Tropical ulcers had appeared soon after our arrival in Thailand and on commencing work in the jungle. The ulcers first attacked the feet and legs, mainly the legs, of the men working in the jungle; there were not many ulcers on people's arms and hands.

At first ulcers were thought to be jungle sores, as sores on the skin were fairly commonplace, owing to the general lack of suitable washing facilities. The only treatment that was provided consisted of wrapping the affected part in cloth soaked in salt solution.

After a while the doctors found that bathing the ulcer and treating it with saline solution had little or no effect. The next trial for a cure was the use of maggots to clear up the large amount of pus formed in the ulcer. In some cases this halted the growth of the ulcer, but no cure was effected.

The Japanese seemed equally at a loss on how to treat these ulcers, and gradually the ulcers enlarged themselves. When they were small the men went out to work, and it was not until they became large that the men were hospitalized.

I developed a small ulcer on my right foot just behind my toes. When it was the size of a pin head, I decided that the current treatment was not producing results. I remembered that during the Spanish Civil War there had been reports that men who had serious wounds on their limbs had had the limb encased in plaster, and left unattended. In many cases the wounded soldiers took a long time to reach a hospital and when the plaster was removed the wound had started to heal.

Amongst my few possessions was a tin of Elastoplast with three or four pieces still left. I put one of these pieces on the cleaned ulcer and left it there until it dropped off through wear. To my delight the ulcer had healed, although it left a discoloration on my foot that lasted for several years.

The Japanese by now had made one or two hospital camps near the base of the railway; these were at Kanchanaburi and Chungkai. When, and in what order they were built, was not known. The men suffering from bad ulcers were sent to these camps, and eventually we met up with them again when we too were evacuated to a hospital in these camps.

The spread of enteric diseases was undoubtedly caused by poor hygiene in the camp. Latrines were dug and consisted of trenches ten feet deep by three feet wide and about thirty feet long. Three bamboos were placed side by side straddling the trench, to make a foothold. Two of these footholds were placed one foot apart and provided a platform; you walked on to the bamboo supports and squatted down. This was reasonably easy if you were healthy and it was daylight. At night it could be hazardous, especially if you lost your footing. If you were weak from illness it was no easy task.

In the camp hospital hollow bamboos were used as bedpans, but as they were only three inches wide at a maximum, juggling with them on a *chang* was achieved with difficulty.

Apart from the primitive latrines the lack of a sufficient supply of water did not allow hands to be washed with any great regularity. The Muslim rule of one hand, the right, for clean actions, and one hand, the left, for dirty actions, was realized to be a very good health rule. Unfortunately the rule was not always obeyed.

By now our clothes were beginning to wear out. Few POWs had arrived in Thailand with more than two sets of clothes. Tropical clothes are light and shirts, trousers, shorts and underwear do not weigh much. There was nothing with which to carry out repairs so gradually everyone started to look very ragged. The Japanese did not provide clothes and we had no spare clothes in our equipment left behind at Non Pladuk.

Boots and shoes also wore out, and several men were now working bare foot; this, of course, hastened the onset of ulcers. Caps had been lost or worn out. The result was a collection of men, some barefoot, some stripped to the waist, few with hats or caps – all toiling in the tropical sun.

This lack of attire, for some unknown reason, used to annoy the Japanese soldiers, who were fussy about personal dress and cleanliness. They commented on uncut finger nails and toe nails and any general lack of personal cleanliness.

The weaker members of the battalion had begun to succumb to the various illnesses that were prevalent in the camp. The Japanese could recognize ulcers, and possibly fevers, as genuine sickness, but were not very impressed by intestinal complaints.

Ulcer patients were evacuated when their condition became serious, but the sufferers of intestinal complaints were often forced back to work because the guards thought they were malingering, consequently they became seriously ill and died. The men who died were buried near the camp, with a service held by one of the padres.

The Roman Catholic padre knew all his flock and when one of them died he officiated at the simple ceremony; all other POWs were buried by the Anglican padre. A record of all deaths was kept by the adjutant, including date and place, for future War Office records. Clothes and other belongings of the dead were passed on to the most needy in the camp, and remained the sole source of supply for some time. The number of deaths at this stage was small.

As the battalion had lost men by death and evacuation, the numbers were made up by the arrival of some Dutch troops. These troops had originally been captured in Java and some detachments had arrived while we were still in Changi.

Having talked with these troops in Changi we were aware of the difference between Dutch and Hollander. All Eurasians in the Dutch East Indies were citizens of the Dutch Empire and were called Dutch. People of European extraction, and hence probably born in Holland, were called Hollanders. But a Hollander could be born in Java or elsewhere in the East Indies, and was still a Hollander; he could be irritated by being called Dutch.

The Dutch army provided us with two amenities, the first of which was spare clothing. Unfortunately, most of the Dutch army were slim and small, so when we were given some spare clothing it did not fit all that well. I acquired a pair of jungle green shorts which were too small to wear with comfort but held together by a piece of string – as the buttons certainly would never meet – did provide an element of decency.

The second amenity was the art of the bottle. Ever since we had been in Thailand there had been no issue of paper, although officers were still charged for this luxury. The supply we had brought up from Malaya was now getting low. From the point of view of smoking it did not matter too much as we were able to procure at different times a supply of Thai cigarettes. From the point of latrine hygiene it was causing some trouble. A careful use of the empty cigarette packets did help, but the supply was inadequate. So we learnt from the Dutch the art of the bottle.

All it required was a bottle, about the size of a soft drink bottle, and strangely enough some came to hand. Grasping the bottle with one hand a stream of water was directed between the legs from the back; the other hand was used to wipe one's bottom.

To begin with we were not over experienced and usually finished up with a bootful of water and no obvious success. However, practice made us proficient and eventually we came to realise what a boon this was to sufferers of dysentery. Talking with the Dutch, we learnt that in the East Indies all WCs are equipped with a stream of water and a towel, and no paper. Thereafter, for the rest of our stay as POWs the bottle was always used in preference to paper.

Shortly after the arrival of the Dutch I became friendly with a Dutch doctor who was the son of a Hollander father and a Javanese mother. He was a well educated man and extremely interesting as a companion. One of his interests was hypnosis.

The camp had no supplies of anaesthetics, either local or general. One of the difficulties this caused was the extraction of teeth; we had no dentist so the doctors coped as well as they could. The Dutch doctor offered his services and hypnotized the patients before an extraction; his services were also occasionally used for minor surgical operations.

I was extremely interested in hypnosis, having seen the doctor in action, so I asked him 'Do you use language to hypnotize a person?' He replied 'No, you hypnotize by thought.' I required proof of this, so I asked him if he would undertake an experiment, with me as an observer. He agreed and I asked him what languages he spoke.

He told me he could speak English, Dutch, Malay, and Javanese. He did not speak Japanese and did not know more than the few necessary words to obey military and other commands. We walked to the perimeter wire and there was one of the guards walking between the wire and the enclosing jungle. This was a space about forty yards wide, and the guard was marching up and down, keeping nearer to the jungle than to the barbed wire.

This situation would allow an ideal experiment to be set up. I said to the doctor 'Can you make the Japanese soldier believe that a snake has fallen from a tree and has coiled itself round his right arm?' I chose the right arm because Japanese soldiers march with their rifles on their right shoulder. 'No problem' he replied, and just stared at the Japanese soldier.

After a minute the soldier went mad. He threw down his rifle, drew his bayonet and struck at his right arm, with the bayonet held in his left hand. At the same time he was calling out in a loud voice to the rest of the guards in the guard hut. They came tumbling out and stared at him in astonishment, then they laughed and called him a fool. Obviously they were telling him that there was no snake. The incident ended with bad tempers all round, so the doctor and I beat a hasty retreat. My experiment had worked. Without the use of language the Japanese soldier had been made to believe exactly what I had requested; I was duly impressed with the doctor's hypnotic powers. He did say, however, that hypnosis would not work on a strong minded person.

Because of sickness in the camp, the work on the railway began to fall behind schedule. The Japanese engineers were worried and the command of the day was 'speedo, speedo' and all ranks were forced to work harder.

The Japanese realized that the harder work required more food, so the ration of rice went up to a staggering one and a half pounds a day. Extra rice was distributed to the working parties in the form of rice balls, with extra salt added to replace that lost in sweating.

In spite of the extra ration of rice the troops were still hungry, requiring meat in their diet. While working in the jungle some wild animals were seen and with a little ingenuity were caught. Whatever was caught was cooked and eaten. We ate snakes and lizards as the easiest catch; some of the Dutch managed to catch the odd monkey and these too were eaten. I did not really enjoy snake, but when cooked and mixed with a little rice, the thought of the animal was put behind you and the meal was enjoyed. Presumably there were plants that were edible, but our knowledge of the plant life in this type of jungle was strictly limited. We could not find any fruit trees and had no idea whether there were roots that could be eaten, so apart from the occasional wild animal we were reduced to eating the normal revolting rations.

One day we were ordered back before the usual end of the day. When we arrived at the camp we saw four or five POWs with their hands tied behind their backs, and all roped together. They all looked filthy and unkempt, with unshaven faces.

The battalion was paraded and the prisoners exhibited. A Japanese officer, through the medium of our interpreter, announced that these POWs were prisoners who had attempted to escape from their camp further up the river. According to the officer they had been caught only a few days after their attempt. They had not been able to find food and we were not sure whether they had been captured trying to get food at a camp or from villagers in the area. Whatever way they had been captured, their period of escape had been limited.

The battalion was informed that the Japanese High Command were very incensed that prisoners should betray the kindness of the Japanese army when they were good enough to look after surrendered personnel. For their crime of escaping, the prisoners were to be taken to the base camp and would receive a severe punishment. We never heard of them again and never knew their fate. This was probably the only attempt to escape from Thailand – at least it was the only one that we heard of.

The clothing situation was now getting worse, so requests were made to the Japanese engineers for some help. It was no use asking our guards for clothes as any information they gave to the Japanese headquarters would never be taken into account. Some more Dutch army kit was made available and also, to our delight, some brown trilby hats. The hats were new and therefore in good condition. They did not fit everybody, but a few lucky ones, including myself, became the proud possessor of a brand new brown trilby hat. Worn with our ragged tropical gear the hats did cause some amusement.

Some footwear also appeared; these were Japanese issue boots, with rubber soles and canvas uppers. Unlike European boots, they had a separate entry for the big toe, similar to a mitten with a place for the thumb. Unfortunately most of the boots supplied were too small for the British troops, although the Dutch troops managed better, as their feet were generally smaller. Another source of footwear came from local sources in the shape of *terompak*. These are similar to the rubber flip-flops used in Britain.

A *terompak* has a wooden sole and a broad canvas band for gripping the foot just behind the toes. Walking in this form of footwear required a little practice, but they were extremely useful in preventing cuts on the foot. Troops who did not receive Japanese issue boots or *terompak*, and had lost their boots, were forced to continue to work barefoot.

Living conditions had now become very monotonous. The working parties went out seven days a week and, because of the speed needed by the engineers, occasionally worked longer hours. The diet was particularly monotonous and unpalatable and the accommodation was poor. The only good point was the dry climate.

The battalion lost count of the days or even weeks. Its constitution was changing as sick were evacuated and reinforcements took their place. Morale was low to say the least.

# CHAPTER VI

# The river of no return

One evening, on returning to camp, I was called by the colonel into his tent. As my company was now seriously depleted I was going to be detached with forty men and sent to another camp.

I chose forty of my gunners, those who were the fittest, to go with me, because nobody knew where the camp was going to be, or what work would have to be done.

The next day we paraded for roll call, complete with our personal belongings, and set off with two Japanese guards. We marched about three to four kilometres up the road to a camp with tents and found we were down by the River Kwai.

The camp had Japanese guards and engineers; across the river was a sawmill, which we could hear was busy working. Language was a problem as we had no interpreter and only one engineer spoke a little English, sufficient to give simple commands.

Our work consisted of felling trees and working with the elephants to get the trees down to the river and then across the river, using a launch, to the sawmill. Only the Japanese went across the river; we were kept strictly on our side and were not allowed to communicate with the troops operating the sawmill. We had cross-cut saws, axes, and machetes which were used to clear the undergrowth so that we could work on the trees. An engineer came with us when we went out to work and indicated which trees were to be cut down. Having cut down a tree it was sawn into lengths for the elephants to carry away.

Not long after we arrived at the camp, some of my gunners were taken away to Hin Tok, a work camp further up the railway line, to work on blasting in the big cutting. They obviously made a success of their work as some more were taken away and replaced with local labourers.

In the camp I was in charge of all aspects of life. I was in charge of roll call, then of the working party and when we got back to camp I had to organize cooking, camp fatigues, and report to the guards. Every soldier went out on the working parties because we were still healthy enough to work.

After a fairly short period all my gunners were replaced by local labourers, each British gunner being replaced by two labourers. They were a mixed collection, mainly recruited from Malaya. I now had eighty men, of whom fifty or so were Malays; the rest included Tamils, Punjabis, and seven men from French Indo-China.

Malay became the *lingua franca* of the camp, and was spoken by the Tamils and some Punjabis. The remainder of the Punjabis spoke Urdu, so I communicated with them in that language. The Indo-Chinese spoke pidgin French, which I found easy enough to make myself understood. Pidgin French was a delightful language. It had eliminated almost all the grammatical rules of French and a conversation would take place on the following lines:

'*Demain Ngien travailler, non?*' ('Will Ngien go out working tomorrow?')
'*Non, Ngien inalade.*' ('No Ngien is ill.')
'*Mais hier sain.*' ('But yesterday he was well.')
'*oui hier Ngien OK, aujourd'hui malade, demain non travailler.*' ('Yes, yesterday Ngien was well, today he is sick, tomorrow he will not be working.')

Communication with the guards was mainly in Japanese, mixed with a little of the Anglo-Japanese we had all learned. As I had to cope with details of work, food, and camp hygiene, my Japanese vocabulary expanded fairly rapidly.

Being in charge of the labourers I had the luxury of a tent to myself. After the crowded conditions back in Tonchan South this was very enjoyable to begin with. With the arrival of the local labourers it proved a lonely existence.

I fed with the labourers and the rations were slightly different from those in the main camp. We no longer had gas-cape greens, but other types of dried vegetables. We still had Number 2 fish. The cooks – from among the labourers – seemed to make a better job of preparing food because I don't remember disliking my meals quite so much.

During this time I spoke no English at all, and hardly had any conversations, except in Malay, so it was mainly a routine of sleeping, eating, and working.

I enquired of the Malays how they came to be working on the railway. They said Japanese government officials had come to the *kampongs* (Malay villages) and told them there was work with good pay in Thailand. They were to leave their families in Malaya and the Japanese would give part of their pay to the families and they would receive the rest.

As none of them received very much pay they presumed their families were getting the difference. If sufficient people did not volunteer to go to Thailand the officials forcefully recruited others to make up the numbers.

All of the Asians in the camp had come from larger camps on the railway line. They told me that conditions were bad, the food was poor, the same food as we were now eating, and that there were little or no medical facilities.

We certainly had none in our detached camp and, because of the lack of medical care, many of the Asians had died from the usual diseases prevalent in the camps, such as malaria, dysentery and chronic ulcers. Each camp occupied by the labourers had lacked any form of organization – which possibly accounted for the greater number of deaths. Later reports suggested that half the labourers brought to Thailand died from hardship and sickness.

Shortly after the gunners and I had arrived at the sawmill camp, the weather changed. There were low, heavy black clouds, promising rain. The air was oppressive and humid, making working unpleasant. We could bathe, however, as the river was by the camp, and the guards did not object to our going down to the river as long as we did not communicate with the troops – whom I now knew to be Australians – at the sawmill.

Within a week or so the rains started, really heavy tropical downpours which soaked us and the ground. The earth became muddy and felling trees was dangerous because the earth was so slippery, particularly on the hilly sections of the ground.

The river started to rise and we could see trees and other vegetation floating down the river. It was now flowing very fast and the launch had difficulty getting the felled tree trunks across to the sawmill. Whether it rained hard, just drizzled, or was fine, the working parties set off every morning to do their stint of tree felling. Usually the rain set in after midday, so at least the morning was fine and allowed felling to go on uninterrupted.

One morning we paraded as usual but the engineers seemed to have a problem. The working party was detailed to set off with one of the Malays in charge and I was told to stay back. Then, after a lot of discussion, one of the engineers told me to accompany him across the river. The previous day had been normal. The Australians who worked at the sawmill had been singing at night, a custom in which they indulged periodically.

The Japanese engineer and I went across the river in a launch and I had my first view at close hand of the sawmill camp. The Australians lived in a large bell tent that was in better condition than most of the tented accommodation given to POWs. When Japanese and I went into this tent we saw a horrifying sight: there were fifteen Australians and thirteen of them were dead. I was staggered as only the night before they had all sounded full of life. We looked at the two men still alive; one was obviously near death and the other was very ill. The Japanese engineer asked me what I thought had happened. I told him I had no idea because I had never seen anything like it, particularly the speed at which it had happened. I suggested we ought to get some medical opinion and that the man still alive, but not the one near death, should be taken to the nearest camp to be seen by a doctor.

He agreed it was no use taking the man who was dying because the men had to be carried to the nearest camp with a doctor. More Japanese soldiers were brought across the river, and the least sick man was put on a stretcher. We had to handle him carefully because he was vomiting and having diarrhoea, both at the same time.

Some of the labourers were brought back from the working party and a stretcher party was formed. With a guard they set off from the camp and we remained waiting anxiously to hear what was the cause of the sickness.

The Japanese engineer and I went back across the river to the sawmill, to the Australians tent; the last one had now died. Studying the men lying on their beds I saw that all of them looked extremely emaciated and drawn up with their knees near their chins. They appeared to be nothing but skin and bone – and all this had happened in twelve or so hours. I could not think what had caused such a transformation from reasonably healthy adults to living skeletons in such a short time. I knew the onset of disease was much quicker in the tropics than in temperate climates, but this transformation was incredible.

Late in the afternoon the answer came back; the man had survived until he reached the doctors but had died shortly after. He had died from cholera. There was consternation in the camp, with Japanese running everywhere and talking excitedly. This was the first incident of the cholera epidemic of 1943. The next day a team of Japanese doctors arrived and gave all the Japanese personnel cholera injections. The labourers did not receive any injections, and neither did I as I was counted with the labourers.

The whole day was spent in clearing our camp so that there was no sign of rubbish anywhere. Stones were collected from the river bank and put under the *changs* in the Japanese tents; cleanliness was the order of the day.

Some of the labourers and I were sent back across the river to clear up the sawmill camp. We buried the Australians in a communal grave, not even knowing who they were. The tent and all the equipment in it were burnt so that the whole area was free from contamination. The Japanese were so afraid of cholera that they insisted on a total clearance of the site.

After two days of clearing up work was resumed on tree felling. The tree trunks were piling up by the sawmill which was now silent because there were no troops to operate it. There was much activity amongst the engineers because railway construction was slowing down from the lack of logs to make the bridges. In the camp we were totally isolated from any news or information so had no idea of how the Japanese intended to get work moving again. We just continued to cut logs and pile them up at the sawmill.

One morning I woke up with stomach pains and diarrhoea. After breakfast I paraded as usual and we set off to work. My diarrhoea was now becoming worse and I kept leaving the working party to squat down by the nearest tree.

The guards observed my behaviour and the guard in charge came up to me and asked '*You byoki desukah?*' (Are you ill?')

I replied '*Byoki desu*' ('Yes'). So I was sent back to our camp with one of the guards. He told the engineer in charge who asked if I had cholera. I told him I thought so and he said I was to go to the main camp. Accordingly, they packed up my few belongings, put my pack on my back, cut a bamboo stick for me and put me on the road, pointing in the right direction for the main camp. By now it had started to drizzle and the road was very muddy and slippery. I slid on the uneven road but slowly made my way back stopping at nearly every third or fourth tree, either to relieve my bowels or to vomit. It was definitely cholera.

I staggered along the road and it began to get dark; the rain continued, by now becoming heavier. But I did not really notice the rain – I was just intent on making that camp, which was three kilometres away. When I did reach it it was night. Because of the rain no guards were visible and everybody else was fast asleep in their tents.

I knew where the hospital tents were and could recognize them because they had *changs* and no other tents were so equipped. I made my way to one of them, crept inside, and saw an empty space near the entrance. I put my pack under the *chang* and collapsed alongside another patient. There I became unconscious, utterly exhausted.

I probably lay on the *chang* for about three days, causing consternation in the camp. At morning roll call both the troops on parade and the sick in hospital were counted. The tally showed one extra prisoner and the adjutant could not account for him; it took about two days before I was recognized as the person surplus to establishment. In the meantime I had been cared for by the few hospital orderlies and when I awoke the cholera had gone. But I was very weak and had difficulty coping with the food – rice porridge and a little fish.

By now there were other cholera patients in the hospital and deaths started to occur. The camp at Tonchan South was lucky in having a doctor who belonged to the Indian Medical Service and thus had some knowledge of the disease and the methods of treating it.

This knowledge did not do a lot of good because there were no suitable drugs available. The main cause of death from cholera is dehydration which is severe. This dehydration causes the patients to shrivel to skin and bone and gives the awful appearance of the patient arching his back and contorting into a writhing posture.

To keep a patient alive a continuous saline drip is needed, but the camp did not possess the equipment to do this. Injections of sterile saline solution were given by hypodermic syringe, but this was usually insufficient to prevent the extreme dehydration.

Only about one-tenth of cholera patients survived. Some died quickly while others lingered on for some time. Why some survived while others died was never clear, as all received the same treatment – little as it was.

When the cholera epidemic became firmly established in the camp the doctors established a form of barrier nursing. Firstly a special area was designated for cholera. Patients suffering from other diseases were segregated to reduce the chance of transmitting the infection. The doctor and a few medical orderlies looking after the cholera patients used a special entrance to the area. There they stripped naked and put on shorts or, of all things, a swimming costume. The doctor wore wellington boots and the orderlies used *terompak*. After finishing a tour of duty the doctor and the orderlies returned to the entrance, stripped naked, bathed again, and then put on their normal attire.

This procedure reduced the risk of contaminating the rest of the camp, although both the doctor and the orderlies were at great risk of contracting the disease. However, they all survived the epidemic by a strict adherence to the conduct laid down by the Indian Medical Service doctor.

The troops were not so lucky; at least one hundred and fifty died from cholera – nearly one-third of the battalion. The epidemic was by now widespread and in other camps up to one-half were dying.

The question was what to do with the corpses; preferably they should have been burnt. Cholera is a water-borne disease, and burying the dead infects the ground. In the monsoon season the ground is soaked and the water drains into the rivers, carrying the cholera bacteria with it. This is probably the reason that Hindus cremate their dead, as cholera is indigenous in the Ganges delta; from there it spreads over India. But it is not necessarily a tropical disease; troops from India took the bacteria home to Britain where it flourished in cities with poor sanitation. In fact many people in the nineteenth century died of cholera contracted from London sewers.

In a cholera epidemic the first step in hygiene is to boil all water for twenty minutes in order to kill the bacteria. This was not possible for all personnel in the battalion as there were insufficient utensils available to boil water for everybody. Tin water that could be boiled was used for the decontamination of the hospital staff, to provide sterile water for the saline solutions used in injections, and for the hygiene of the cooks and cooking utensils.

The rest of the troops and officers had to forego washing and cleaning teeth for the whole of the period of the epidemic. Unfortunately, when I left the sawmill camp I did not take my petrol tin with me, so I could not boil water for the use of the officers in the tent. This lack of personal washing in turn produced other problems, mainly skin infections, including ulcers.

As soon as I was fit enough, I was discharged from the hospital to make room for the ever increasing demand from new cholera patients. I returned to the officers' tent and convalesced as best I could on the rations. We now had a Japanese sergeant in charge of the guards and of the camp. His rank in the Japanese army was *gunso*.

He was much better than the previous guard commanders and agreed to the POWs going down to buy food from the Thai traders who came up the River Kwai on barges. My knowledge of Thai now stood me in good stead; the *gunso* was informed that I spoke Thai and so I was sent off to trade with the barges on the river.

The *gunso* had seen service in Java so spoke Malay. This, too, was fortunate because when we lost our interpreter I became interpreter to the camp speaking Malay. By now the constitution of the battalion had altered so much that we had lost the volunteers from Malaya, leaving me as the only Malay speaker.

★   ★   ★

Perhaps now is the time to say a little more about the *gunso*. With a rank equivalent to a sergeant, he was a sufficiently high ranking NCO to be in charge of 600 POWs. His name was Oburi, addressed as *Oburi gunso*, and his service in Java had been with front-line troops, fighting the Dutch Army to capture the island. I gathered he had also performed some garrison duties in Java, but never found out why he had been put in charge of a POW camp in Siam.

He was a sturdy, thick-set man of average height and grizzled appearance, able to support a good growth of stubble when he omitted to shave. I put his age at early to middle fifties, but it was difficult for us to estimate Japanese ages; they seemed to look the same for years and then suddenly become old. In addition, wartime experiences tended to age a man beyond his years.

To begin with our relationship was limited to discussing orders for railway work, sick troops, rations and the various minor incidents of camp life. As time went on, more general talk came after the formal discussions. On my part, the talking was somewhat guarded, because of the considerable differences in national cultural background.

I had learnt several aspects of the difficulties encountered in the Japanese language; The Japanese for 'Is there/have you got' is *arimasukah*, but I learnt the hard way when asking 'Gunso arimasukah?' (Is the *gunso* around?) as the verb was used only with inanimate objects. My query inferred that the *gunso* was an object – to which the Japanese soldiers took exception. The correct question was 'Gunso orimasukah?' when referring to humans. Small linguistic difficulties such as this made one careful with one's utterances; a vowel could make a difference!

One morning I was summoned to the guard tent to be confronted by a highly enraged guard and the *gunso*. The guard had found a Chinese newspaper cartoon that showed a large hand grasping two chopsticks, with the upper one labelled with the Chinese flag and the lower one with the Japanese flag. As the upper chopstick is moved to push the food against the lower one, the inference was obviously that the Chinese were hammering the Japanese.

I had no idea how the cartoon could have got into the camp, and said so. The *gunso* said we would investigate the affair, and dismissed the guard. When he had gone the *gunso* said 'very funny, but the artist forgot that the upper chopstick has to move up and down, while the lower one remains firm'.

Luckily the *gunso* had a good sense of humour, so we both laughed off that episode – but it could have been a nasty encounter.

Little by little the *gunso's* background came to light in our general conversations. He was a regular soldier and had fought in China before being sent to Java, but had not fought in Malaya. He had a wife and two children in Japan, and complained he had not seen his wife for seven years. Maybe it had only seemed like seven years as, presumably, he had passed through Japan on his way to Java from China.

I had the feeling that he wanted to talk with us rather than with the guards, because he considered us front-line soldiers and the guards just POW watchers. It is true we had committed the unforgivable sin of surrendering, but he appreciated we had been ordered to surrender rather than doing it on our own volition.

It was with Oburi that we had discussed the disciplinary methods of the Japanese army, as described previously. Oburi was a good disciplinarian, and kept the guards well under control. Face slapping was reduced to a complete minimum and towards the end of our stay in Tonchan South, practically vanished.

Oburi gradually became friendly towards the officers, and visited us frequently in our tent. One of the reasons for describing him in some detail is that his life and mine were curiously entwined; later, he saved my life.

★   ★   ★

While I was still convalescing I started my new jobs of interpreter and trader with the barges. Because the battalion had lost so many troops from the cholera epidemic, reinforcements appeared. These included Dutch, British, Australian, and even a few Americans who had been captured from naval vessels fighting in the Dutch East Indies. One of these Americans was a naval officer who came to live in our tent, and from him we learned of the battles in the Coral Sea, and the odds against which they had had to fight.

The working parties were now facing even more difficult conditions. Working in the rain was unpleasant and caused more sickness. The earth was that much heavier to dig and carry and the work under construction could be washed away by the rain.

One night there was an exceptionally heavy storm and the whole camp was woken by the guards well before the normal time of roll call. The command was '*oru men* and *oru elephanto*' ('all men and all elephants'). All the men who were not desperately ill in the hospital were paraded and marched off to a gulley some distance from the camp.

The heavy rain had washed away some of the soil and all the uprights for the bridge across the gulley had collapsed like a pack of cards and were lying one on top of the other. We thought this was going to be a very lengthy operation, but no, the engineers had a solution. Ropes were tied around the uprights and all the men and all the elephants pulled as hard as they could. Very slowly, all the timbers came upright into their correct position, and were as they had been erected. The engineers then hurriedly produced some rails and laid them across the horizontal beams of the uprights. An engineer then went across on each side of the bridge and hammered in nails to fix the rails to the horizontal beams. When the engineers had finished they had a bridge with a set of rails across it but we hoped we would never be on a train crossing that particular bridge.

The work of repairing the bridge was finished by the end of the morning and we returned to camp for a belated breakfast. In the afternoon the working parties went out again on their normal tasks.

At that stage of the railway construction the repaired bridge was adequate; there was little traffic on the line as yet. The Japanese had adapted lorries to travel on the rails by removing the road wheels and replacing them with flanged railway wheels. These lorries were light enough to go over the repaired bridge without doing any damage. Occasionally, a lorry would tow a couple of railway wagons and this, too, did not affect the bridge.

Besides the work on the railway there was another unpleasant task, which was the burying of the dead. We had considerable numbers in the camp who needed to be buried, and the Japanese did not want to spare too many men on this task as the railway had precedence.

We would have preferred to burn the corpses, but it was hard enough trying to get enough dry wood for the cooking fires and the fires to provide boiled water for the hospital. The wood was damp from the rains and in any case cremation would have to take place in the open, with the very likely occurrence of rain to make it impossible.

The solution was communal graves. A large pit was dug and the dead thrown in. Individual graves were not allowed because that would mean clearing more jungle to make space for the graves. The pits were gradually filled with the dead and earth piled on top; presumably the adjutant kept records of who was buried and where.

Not only did we have to cope with our own dead but one day we were detailed as a burial party to go to a labourers' camp. It was impossible to count the number of dead, as they were lying everywhere. All of the deaths were from cholera, and it looked as if more than half the camp had died. We estimated at least two hundred dead, and having dug a pit, the bodies were thrown into it. When all had gone in we shovelled earth on top. By now it was getting dusk but just as we thought we had finished we saw the odd hand still sticking up through the earth. More earth was thrown on top and padded down. Only then could men and guards return wearily back to camp.

In between going on these burial parties I went down to the river to meet the Thai trading barges. Standing by the bank I could see that the river was still swollen with the heavy rains. In addition to the trees that were floating down the stream, there were now bodies, presumably of cholera victims; the water from the river was definitely unsafe for any purpose unless it had been thoroughly boiled.

Apart from cholera the troops still suffered from the original complaints. Malaria had become worse as the mosquitoes had increased with the rains. Tropical ulcers had also increased as the wet conditions hastened the onset of sores and other skin diseases.

One of the skin diseases now appearing was scabies, caused no doubt by the lack of washing facilities. I found that I had this intensely irritating disease and went to see the doctor. He had nothing to cure it, but suggested some treatment.

The Japanese had organized a supply of electricity by wires stretched along wooden poles running by the side of the road. The voltage was high and the conducting wires were mounted on porcelain insulators; inside the insulators were blocks of sulphur.

Sulphur was the required cure for scabies. At night we crept out of the camp, past the guards, and shinned up the electricity poles. Taking great care, we lifted the porcelain insulators and took out the block of sulphur. We then returned quietly to the camp.

The next step was to purchase some red palm oil or coconut oil. The sulphur was then scraped thinly and put into the oil. When the preparation was complete, the next thing was to borrow an old petrol can to boil some water.

Everything was now ready for the cure. With the aid of a friend you stripped off all your clothes, which were put into the boiling water and continued to be boiled. This did not improve the clothes but was essential to get rid of the scabies mites.

The last piece of equipment was a nail brush and some soap. The skin was now scrubbed with the brush and soap until all the scabies pustules bled. This was not too bad on the back but the belly was more painful and on the scrotum was excruciatingly painful. After scrubbing, the mixture of sulphur and oil was applied to the whole skin. The application produced great irritation, and naked men could be seen jumping up and down, swearing like troopers, as the sulphur got to work. When the irritation had died down, and the clothes had dried, you could dress again, ready for the next round.

This treatment had to be repeated for three days running, after which you could assume you had conquered the scabies mite. Care had to be taken not to become reinfected. I managed the treatment and, fortunately, did not have a recurrence in that camp. The main object of eliminating scabies was to avoid the complication of sceptic scabies which was more difficult to treat. The *gunso* connived at men leaving the camp to get the sulphur and the guards did not stop them. He probably realized that curing the disease was essential to keeping the troops working; this was another example of his enlightened control of the camp.

I had one more bout of skin disease. At night I started to itch at the base of my stomach. No amount of scratching seemed to alleviate the itch, so off to the doctor once more. I described the complaint and he said 'Lower your shorts and I'll have a look at it'. I did so and he burst out laughing and said 'You've got crabs – pubic lice to the uninformed – and there's not a woman within fifty miles of the camp. After this I'll believe in the lavatory seat theory of the propagation of venereal diseases.'

I said that was all very well but what was he going to do about my crabs. 'Simple' said he, 'fetch me your razor'. And with that he shaved off all the pubic hairs. A thorough wash with some boiled water and soap, and once again I could face the world without itching.

Shortly after this incident the Japanese decided to do something about our health and produced smallpox vaccine. We were all duly vaccinated, although there never had been any sign of smallpox. It was just a gesture by the Japanese Higher Command to show they were taking care of us.

Now that the news of the cholera epidemic had percolated through to Japanese headquarters, it was decided that POWs should be tested for the disease. Japanese doctors appeared and proceeded to give the glass rod test★ to all personnel. We were accustomed to this treatment but after a while the Japanese ran out of glass rods so improvised with bamboo sticks. This test was most unpleasant, particularly if the bamboo had any splinters on it. The results of these tests never became known, so probably it was just another public relations effort.

The Japanese in the camp had realized the necessity for boiling water. They brought fifty-gallon oil drums to their hutted camp, and used them for boiling water. The drums were filled with water, the POWs supplied wood for the fire, and the Japanese enjoyed hot baths everyday. We were duly envious.

By strict adherence to the hygiene rules the incidence of cholera now fell. The troops continued on working parties, but the insistence on speed was reduced and the work became slightly easier. The railway had advanced nearer to Tonchan and the trains provided a better supply of food.

This gave the officers less work to do and more time was spent in our tents. When work was slack the hours were spent in conversation, there being no

---

★ As explained in Chapter I this involves thrusting the glass rod up the anus, giving it a twirl to remove some faeces, then making a faecal smear on a glass dish.

alternative for passing the time. Discussion seemed to be led by the Catholic padre, and the other officers joined in.

Naturally enough with the padre a common topic was religion. The arguments were lengthy because both officers and men had developed an antipathy to the efforts of the priests in camp. The officers tended to agree with the troop's description of padres as 'God botherers'. Perhaps it was not entirely the padres' fault, as there was not much spiritual comfort they could give to the troops, considering the conditions under which we all lived.

The padre insisted that if we had faith we would survive, implying that it was his particular brand of faith. Two of us, the doctor and I, said in that case the survival rate should be higher amongst Catholics than other believers or non-believers, whereas the statistics of death did not support the belief in his faith.

On looking at the men who died there was no apparent pattern, and disease and death were indiscriminate in their incidence. We had one or two officers who had worked in the East for some time and they proffered their knowledge of other religions in that region. None of the religions seemed to offer any explanation of why some died and some lived; it did not appear to depend on their actions or their beliefs. All afflictions had a random distribution, although individual actions could have a bearing on the incidence.

The Buddhist religion states that all men are responsible for their own actions and that was accepted by us as the nearest approach to an answer for the present situation. We were not so sure about the second tenet of Buddhism, that merit or sin determined the future existence in the next incarnation, that *karma* was immortal.

The doctor and I were determined defenders of the concept of random action as this fitted in with the scientific concept of the laws of chaos. If nature could not distinguish between any two electrons at one and the same time, then there would appear to be a parallel case that the recording of the specific actions of any one person should also be in doubt.

Although this argument appealed to us, we acknowledged that religion could provide some comfort to people who did not want to argue for an impersonal approach to the incidents of life. These discussions provided a means of passing the time but never led to any justifiable conclusions. We were now waiting to go on to the next stage of our training as railway builders.

# CHAPTER VII

# I'm dreaming of a white Christmas

Orders came through that the battalion was to be despatched to camps higher up the river. Those considered not fit to march would stay behind, and about one hundred and fifty remained in the camp. We had had so many changes with reinforcements to replace sick personnel that the remainder were a very mixed collection and it was difficult to recognize the original battalion.

After the contingent to go up country had marched out the remainder reorganized the accommodation, giving all of us much more space in the tents. Small working parties were detailed for camp fatigues and, as the health of the POWs improved, outside working parties were once again organized.

The Japanese had been hurrying the construction of the railway again and the track now reached the camp. There was a special force for the actual laying of the track and members of this force passed through our area.

We spoke to the members of the force and realized they were receiving better treatment in the way of food and tented accommodation than we were. We put this down to the force being specially recruited for a specialist job. They also had a detachment of medical staff with them. A party, called K Force, had been assembled to provide medical care for the POW camps in Thailand. This K Force had been split into detachments to accompany the different groups of POWs who had come to Thailand before us.

The track was laid on the earth of the embankments that we had built and also across the bridges that we had constructed. There were passing points made with double tracks; the majority of the line was single track. Presumably there was a method of signalling but we were not aware of it. Telephone communication was apparent as we could receive orders from other areas.

The working parties now being sent out had much lighter work than the work previously allotted to the camp. The embankments, ridges and cuttings were all finished and the task of our parties was just tidying up the track area.

Trains driven by the converted lorries brought material and rations to the camp; the material included ballast. The POWs were issued with pickaxes and they had to lever up the sleepers of the track and put ballast underneath them. At the same time the working party had to lay ballast between the sleepers and level it off; the result was a finished railway, complete with sleepers, rails and ballast. This work was light enough for the troops to recover their health and the number of fit men increased as time went on.

The parties were organized under officers as before; there were six or seven left in the camp besides the Anglican padre, one doctor, and the accountant. The Roman Catholic padre and the other two doctors had accompanied the troops sent up country.

Both the padre and the accountant travelled up the road to other camps, the padre conducting services and the accountant keeping track of the men's wages and producing pay for all of us. As officers we drew our thirty yen a month – the deductions for accommodation, food and paper still being made although nothing was supplied.

Japanese troops were now beginning to use the road, so presumably the way from Thailand to Burma must have been clear. Almost every day a detachment of troops would pass the camp, hauling equipment on two-wheeled, light carts with ropes attached to the carts. These were piled high with sacks and boxes, but it was difficult to see what the contents were. Although the rains had abated the road was muddy and the troop movements made the surface worse.

Many times the carts would get bogged down in the mud and more men were needed to extricate them. This was accompanied by much shouting, with officers and NCOs yelling at the men for a greater effort. There was obviously a need for speed.

Light artillery was also hauled along the road, including ammunition in carts. All of it was shifted by man power; no draught animals were used. The soldiers were armed and, from their appearance, bound for the front in Burma. They had a very long way to go, over three hundred miles to the southern part of Burma, so it seemed a strange way to transport troops.

The railway was not usable for heavy traffic as yet, so marching on foot was the only method of transferring the soldiers from Thailand. The sight of these troop movements cheered us up – if the Japanese army was reduced to moving troops in this fashion, then the war could not be going so well for them. We were also cheered by the sight of Japanese troops being shouted at in the same way as we were shouted at by our guards.

The travels of the padre and accountant to the other camps allowed them to bring back news of the outside world. We learnt that Italy had been invaded and the war was now going well for the Allies. The end of the war seemed a long way off – but at least the news was no longer so discouraging and we had hopes of one day ending our POW existence. Nobody expected to be home by this Christmas, but we thought there was a possibility of the next Christmas. We had no radio in the camp so we were entirely dependent on the padre and the accountant for any news.

The padre, unfortunately, did not have a good memory. I think his experiences had unnerved him to some extent as he was always a very quiet person. To help his memory he used to write down the news on a small piece of paper and hide it under the elastic band that kept up his stockings. He was better clothed than the rest of us because he had not undertaken any physical work or the organization of outside working parties.

Normally the Japanese never interfered with the priests of any denomination, but one day the padre was searched and the paper hidden in his stockings came to light. He did not reappear at the camp for some time and when he did he was quieter than ever. Apparently the Japanese soldiers had obtained from him the source of his news.

This started a thorough searching of all camps and of all accommodation and personnel in the camps. More than one radio was discovered and the Japanese became very angry. The radio operators were caught and paraded round the camps. At our camp in Tonchan South, a Japanese officer, who was the senior interpreter, came to give the officers a lecture which was to be passed on to the troops. He worked himself into a fury about the discovery of the radios, beginning quietly enough emphasising how wicked it was to secrete radios to hear the false propaganda from the Western allies. The Japanese were looking after us so well – with all the usual comments on the fact that POWs were not worthy of such treatment.

As the lecture proceeded his voice rose and he said 'You British think we Japanese bloody fools. You think we do not know what you do. You think we do not know that you are hiding radios. You think we know f★★★ nothing but really we know f★★★ all'. This no doubt was to show off his command of the English idiom; we dared not laugh as that would have been extremely foolish – and dangerous.

From his accent, the Japanese officer must have learnt his English in America which may have explained why he was not conversant with true English idiom. Of all the Japanese with whom we came into contact, his command of English was probably the best.

The Imperial Japanese Army depended on British and other European interpreters for almost all of their communication with the POWs. The majority of the interpreters had been missionaries, or associated with missions, in Japan. Few British people had learnt Japanese at that time.

However, the troops did laugh when we passed on the message, and we enjoyed a chuckle ourselves. But the incident was not without its tragedy; the radio operators were taken away and once again we never knew what happened to them.

The railway traffic was now beginning to increase and the converted lorries on the system were joined by steam locomotives. These were small engines and where they came from was unknown; they were not like either the Malayan or the Thai locomotives, they were much smaller.

This smallness was just as well, because one day, amid great excitement, the Japanese shouted out once again '*Oru men, oru elephanto*'. When we arrived at the scene of the request, we were not happy to see a locomotive that had failed to cross a bridge over a gulley. This was the repaired bridge we had worked on before, when it had collapsed with the heavy rain.

When the locomotive had attempted to cross the bridge, the railway lines had bulged outwards and it had slipped down between the rails. Once again we thought this was going to be an impossible task, but no, the engineers solved it. All the men and all the elephants were used to lift the locomotive, and the lines were hurriedly hammered back into shape. Extra sleepers were produced and placed underneath the rails. The lines were quickly nailed to these sleepers and there was the locomotive once more sitting on the rails. For improvisation we could not fault the Japanese engineers.

All bridges in the area were then strengthened in the same way. We wondered whether similar incidents had happened further up the line because there were many such bridges over gulleys, not to mention viaducts over more difficult terrain.

The incidence of disease had dropped because everyone now knew much more about tropical conditions. Bamboo was avoided as far as possible as we knew that contact with it caused ulcers. Tropical ulcers were becoming rarer; all those suffering from them had been despatched to base camps down the river for hospital treatment. Malaria had also declined as the weather was drier and mosquitoes were fewer. We were left with enteric diseases, and dysentery was the chief complaint.

I was no exception and contracted dysentery – diagnosed as amoebic dysentery – and was duly admitted to hospital. I was put into a small tent which was equipped with a *chang* which I lay on. Treatment was still the little black charcoal pills, but we did have a limited supply of M & B 693, which helped.

During the day the camp was almost deserted, with everybody out at work, and I rested on the *chang*, trying to overcome the dysentery. One morning, as I lay in the tent, an elephant's trunk appeared and the sensitive tip passed up and down over my body. It was shortly joined by another trunk. I lay there mesmerized, wondering whether these were wild elephants investigating the tent. It was probable that they were wild because the domesticated elephants had either moved on to another camp or were at work. What would they do? I was obviously an object of interest to them. They continued, probably for only a few minutes, to investigate me, but it seemed like a lifetime. Eventually they moved off and I was left alone.

Nobody else in the camp had seen the elephants and some of the orderlies thought that I had dreamt up the whole incident. I assured them I had not – I can still see those trunks waving over me, up and down my body, deciding whether I was friend or foe.

After this frightening encounter, when I went down to the Thai barges to trade, I watched the elephants with more interest. Their drivers would bring them down to the river's edge, remove the shackles from their feet, and let them go into the river. They waded out until the water reached their bellies, then they started to squirt water over themselves. When they had finished their bath they came out of the river of their own accord and waited on the bank while their drivers replaced the shackles, then driver and elephant moved off to their camp. The shackles were iron chains, fixed round their legs just above their feet, with one shackle on each leg. The elephants were hobbled by joining the shackles with a chain.

There were several rafts anchored near the river bank with Thai families living on them. This was the place where the trading barges used to tie up. The rafts were made of bamboo and were quite large, about twenty feet wide by fifty feet long.

A hut, also made of bamboo, was built on each raft with a thatched roof of palm leaves, similar to the *atap* roofs in Malaya. The hut was placed in the middle, so that there was quite a large space all around, with more space at the ends than at the sides. The whole family of the owner lived on the raft, and the children could be seen running about. Strangely, none of the children ever fell in the river.

The rafts were tethered to the bank at both ends and, as the river rose or fell, they either moved out into the river or came closer to the bank. In either case, the position of each raft had to be altered to suit the circumstances. If it were too far out, the current imposed too strong a pull on the tethering ropes. If it were too near, it could run aground on the river bank and upset.

The raft dwellers obtained the help of the elephant drivers, and it was very interesting to see them at work. The driver by some means gave a command to the elephant to move the raft, and the elephant instinctively knew whether to push it in or push it out.

It would wade into the river and if it was pushing the raft in towards the bank, the elephant would put its head against the raft and push in the upstream end first. If it had pushed in the downstream end the raft would have been swept out into the river by the current. The elephant received no guidance and appeared to use its own intelligence.

On completing the task of moving the raft the elephant would have a bath, then come out and wait for its shackles to be put back on its legs. I always watched this performance with admiration.

We had just the one doctor in the camp and the Japanese were now supplying some more drugs, including the M&B 693; the presence of these drugs caused some trouble.

The Japanese army supplied brothels and 'comfort girls' for their troops and the troops were supposed to use them, incurring disciplinary action if they did not. The girls were regularly medically inspected and trouble ensued if they became infected. A Japanese soldier suffering from venereal disease was severely disciplined – even executed if the circumstances warranted it.

Our Korean guards had been replaced by Japanese and one of these new guards on his leave in a rest camp, had contracted gonorrhoea by not using the official brothels. He came to the medical officer and intimated he wanted some M&B 693 to cure himself. He was told he could not have any of the drug as the supply was not sufficient for the needs of the camp.

The argument between the doctor and the guard continued for two or three days, by which time the guard was becoming frantic. He threatened the doctor, who in the end had to give in and supply him with some tablets of M&B 693. Now came the interesting bit; the supply of the pills given to the guard was enough to stop his symptoms but for a cure he needed a full course of the medicine, which the doctor did not supply.

The guard was christened 'the Nip with the drip', and we wondered what would happen when his symptoms returned. There was some respite because the symptoms were suppressed for several days. Then fortune smiled on us and the guard, with some of his companions, was transferred to another camp. Once again a story with an unknown ending, but we were getting used to not knowing the outcome of many incidents.

I was continuing to act as interpreter for the camp, and translating the orders of the few remaining engineers, via the *gunso*, to the working parties. Periodically the *gunso* would go down to the base camps by train to enjoy a few comfort girls. He must have had a good time because whenever he returned he was very sleepy for two or three days.

Daring this time the other officers and I became quite friendly with the *gunso* and one day he told me he would like to learn to play bridge. I gathered that the ability to play bridge and golf advanced one's social status considerably in Japan. So here the *gunso* had an admirable opportunity to learn bridge.

I started by teaching him the rudiments of the game in Malay. Then we taught him the numbers in English and also the names of the suits. But trying to get him to understand the aim of the game was laborious, although we succeeded in the end.

Our efforts had other rewards as well, such as a lamp to provide the necessary illumination to play. When he was pleased with his play – and hence grateful – he would produce a tin of condensed milk as a 'presento' to the tent. A tin of condensed milk does not sound much of a gift, but to us it was sheer luxury.

The instruction caused me some amusement, because attempting to translate some words of advice into Malay produced queer results. For instance the following piece of advice sounds quite peculiar in Malay: 'never take jump take-outs in long suits; many suits have been ruined and rubbers lost in this way.' This evoked the question from the *gunso* 'Do I have to jump off my chair?' So I knew that particular piece of advice had not achieved its aim. In the end I gave up trying to provide such pearls of wisdom in Malay.

Most of the soldiers were now working either on outside parties or on fatigues in the camp. This provided them with money to buy food to supplement their rations, and tobacco. We received no cigarette issue in Thailand, unlike in Malaya, so the purchase of tobacco was a necessity.

The health of all the men was improving and when the working parties set off to the railway line the troops used to sing; popular songs were 'Colonel Bogey' and 'Bless them all'.

Due to the easier conditions, better food, and most of them being paid, the troops were also in good spirits. This improvement in outlook appeared to help recovery from illness and the doctor and the rest of us discussed what factors contributed to a person keeping fit under the camp conditions.

I had had a friend in the camp who was a gunner in 18th Division, the force that had arrived in Singapore just in time to be captured. The last contingent arrived only ten days or so before the capitulation. My friend had been a lawyer in a large practice in England and had married the daughter of the head of the firm. He obviously had a bright future before him when he returned to England.

In Singapore and in Thailand he had been the life and soul of the party, always in a good humour and helping his friends when needed. One day he contracted malaria but did not appear to be seriously ill, so probably was suffering from BT malaria, the milder form of the disease. After only seven days, he turned his face to the tent wall and died for no apparent reason.

Perhaps he felt the situation was hopeless and saw no end to his captivity. It could only have been a frame of mind that caused the fatal reaction to the malaria. We had all heard that people in other civilizations could will themselves to die, but we never expected a person from a Western civilization to do just that.

Looking at the men who had survived and those who had died, we decided that one thing of paramount importance was an extended education. The English education system was founded on the idea of '*mens sana in corpore sano*' – a sound mind in a sound body, where the sound body was needed to have the sound mind. Here, under POW circumstances, it appeared that a sound mind was useful in maintaining a sound body, rather than the reverse.

How was a sound mind to be achieved? The mind needed exercise just as the body needs exercise to keep it functioning at its full potential. The only form of mental exercise lay in conversation, because there were no other forms of mental activity available with our limited resources.

An extended education provided topics for discussion, whereas those who could not fall back on such topics were deprived of the opportunity to converse. Trivial topics of general conversation, such as the deeds of the local football club, the weather, the actions of acquaintances, local living conditions, had no content in a POW camp in the jungle. Without such topics of conversation, the mind became dull, and interest in living was lost. It was observed that those who died had slowly become more silent and had lapsed into a state of lethargy.

There were other factors to be taken into consideration, such as whether the person had lived in a town or in the country. Those living in the country were more self reliant and adapted to what was, in effect, country living in a jungle. They expressed greater interest in their surroundings, which provided some exercise for their minds.

The ability to keep alive depended very much on personal hygiene, and here the regular soldiers had an advantage over the conscripts in the army. Ingrained habits from army life were followed by the regulars, even under the most adverse conditions. The attempt to be presentable by looking after cleanliness and clothes helped to maintain good health.

Lastly there was a factor that had nothing to do with mental activity or habit, it was simply a question of food. People of large stature needed more food than people of small stature, so the smaller, more wiry persons had a better chance of survival because all received the same inadequate rations. The rations could almost suffice for those of small stature, but were certainly inadequate for those of large stature and a starvation ration rendered a person more open to disease.

These factors were general trends and the death of some individuals caused us some surprise; there seemed to be no adequate reason for their inability to survive.

# CHAPTER VIII

# Pennies from heaven

The POWS in the camp at Tonchan South had now entered a much improved existence, mainly due to the purchase of food from the trading barges. I had been buying from these barges, using my knowledge of Thai, and now I was also buying for other camps in Tonchan near our own.

As our purchases had increased we used skips to collect the food. A skip was a basket woven from palm leaves and strengthened with bamboo; it was circular in shape with a diameter of about three feet and was about three and a half feet deep. To carry it, a bamboo pole was pushed through the top part of the skip, just below the rim, and the pole was carried on the shoulders of two people, with the skip between them.

Carrying loads in this fashion is a common practice in Asia. For heavy loads the skip with two men is employed. For lighter loads, a pole is carried on the shoulder by one man and the load consists of two parts, one at each end of the pole. The two loads are balanced at both ends by shifting the pole on the shoulder. The use of a pole for carrying heavy loads builds up a pad of muscle where the neck and shoulder meet. When carrying such a load we employed the method used by the local people. You walked with slightly bent knees, taking small steps, and grunting with every stride to avoid rupturing yourself with the weight.

Either two or four of us would set off in the morning to make our way down to the river. The path was hilly and care had to be taken if it was muddy and slippery. Having arrived at the river, I would go aboard the barges to see what each had to offer.

The most important purchase was fruit, because our diet lacked sweetness, and the barge traders had a good selection. I bought limes, Thai oranges which are very sweet, and bananas – usually the small, very yellow ones which are much sweeter than bananas bought in England. There were also pineapples and papayas, both sweet, and pomelos, the latter being like a large grapefruit, but less juicy and not so sweet as the other fruit.

For vegetables there were onions and garlic, both useful to flavour our stews, while Chinese radish and many types of green vegetables were also available. All these made the stews much more appetizing.

For protein I purchased duck eggs and generally bought one thousand at a time. These eggs were counted individually – which improved my counting in Thai considerably. With this buying of eggs went the purchase of oil for frying, usually coconut oil, which was available in tins. Each tin contained four gallons of coconut oil, so it had to be divided up into smaller amounts to be sold to individual members of the camp.

Everyone became expert at making omelettes from duck eggs, usually thickened with a little rice to make a substantial meal. The omelettes were flavoured with onions, garlic, or limes with added sugar.

For sugar I bought gula Malacca, palm sugar, which was brown in colour and similar to very thick treacle. It made an excellent omelette with limes. Palm sugar is prepared by tying the flower at the top of a coconut palm at top and bottom. A slit is made in the enveloping leaves and the flower is beaten with a stick. This causes sap to exude from the flower, and this is then collected in a receptacle.

The receptacle is sterilized with a piece of slaked lime, otherwise the sap ferments and toddy, a very alcoholic drink, is formed. The sap is boiled and, on cooling, forms a treacle-like liquid or a soft, brown solid. Coconuts were also on sale but were not that popular with the troops.

The barges stocked Thai cigarettes which were expensive as far as we were concerned, but were excellent. A cheaper form of tobacco was sold in hanks, with an ounce of tobacco being about a foot square and two inches thick. It was very loose in texture and looked like dried grass, but was quite strong when smoked. The troops nicknamed it 'hag's bush'. Paper could be purchased to roll cigarettes. We could also buy a few luxuries such as soap, a sarong, a good pair of sandals – provided we had the money – but usually food came first.

The accountant and I ran a canteen where all ranks could purchase what they could afford. This needed some choice to be made because the pay would not stretch to everything a person would have liked to buy. The canteen was run at a profit to purchase food, and other odd amenities, for the sick in hospital. They still received neither food for pay, and though we could manage to give them the standard rations from the rations for the whole camp, the extra food was welcome.

Clothing was still short and I was reduced to a sarong, a pair of *teroma pak*, the local wooden sandals and my trilby hat – quite a distinctive costume. I was also becoming well known on the barges as the traders were intrigued by a European speaking Thai.

When buying goods out East conversation starts in a general fashion. There are the usual questions 'Are you married?' 'How many children do you have?' – the latter question being asked irrespective of whether one is married or not. Questions are asked about where you live, how much ground you have, and what kind of house do you live in, all difficult questions to answer against a Thai background. When such questions are finished, haggling over the price of goods can commence.

The same kind of questions could also be posed by Japanese soldiers. The guards would ask POWs when they were working 'You *wifu-kah*' that is 'have you a wife?' If you said no and wore glasses you were likely to get your face slapped. According to the Japanese married men were supposed to wear glasses, but bachelors were not supposed to wear them. We never found out why.

One barge was owned by a young Thai woman, who we all thought was one of the prettiest women we had ever seen. Perhaps that was due to the fact we had not seen any other woman for some considerable time. However, we discovered later that Thai women have a reputation for being beautiful.

She was christened Lulu and I tended to do most of my trading with her. She became very friendly and after I had made my purchases, she would give me a gift of food. This was often a Thai delicacy, some of which were strange to Western tastes, but one dish I came to like was fish fried with sugar, the fish being of the dried variety and possessing a rather gamey taste. For very large purchases Lulu would produce a bottle of Thai whisky, a lethal drink after many months of abstinence, but none the less very enjoyable. If I came with only one helper to carry the goods, then he would be invited aboard too, and enjoy her hospitality. To have this treatment was lucky indeed, as few other POWs could have been so fortunate – and it was all due to learning Thai.

The original reason I had learnt Thai arose when I had been joined in Changi by a friend, Bill Adams, who had been in the same regiment in England. We had gone out together by boat to India, but when we arrived in Bombay he was sent to Malaya to join the staff in Malaya Headquarters, and I was posted to the North-West Frontier in India.

After the capitulation of Singapore he came to join the regiment in the 11th Indian Division area and one day suggested to me that we might try to escape. In order to do so we had to pass through Malaya and Thailand, and then find our way through Burma. He suggested I learnt Malay and Thai so that we would stand a better chance of making our way through the different countries.

Bill started to teach me Thai; he had lived and worked in Thailand for ten years. I continued with the lessons in the Australian area of Changi. Malay I learnt in the 11th Indian Division area; we had several officers there who had previously worked in Malaya and had joined units both as interpreters and to provide local knowledge of the country.

My friend was sent to Thailand with a contingent of POWs before I went to live in Changi village. I eventually saw him in the distance when I was at Kanchanaburi, but we did not have a chance to talk.

I did not meet Bill again until I had returned to England and joined the Far East POW Club. I spent some time with him prior to leaving for Malaya to take up an appointment in the Colonial Civil Service in the middle of 1946.

Although we chatted a lot about POW days, he never told me what he had really been doing in Thailand, and it was only in the nineties that I had a fuller realization of his experiences.

Rations had improved slightly because the railway was providing better transport to our camps; there were additional vegetables for the gascape stew. The Japanese headquarters had obviously decided that the rations must be improved to keep the POWs from falling sick, so they sent up local cattle which were called yaks by the troops. These were the humped-back Indian variety, smaller than English cattle, and with thin legs.

A herd of yaks would pass by the camp practically every day, but none stopped to be given to our camp. The *gunso* must have inquired why we did not receive any cattle. He told me that, because we were part of the Singapura group, we were not going to get any. As we did not get yaks, neither did our guards.

The *gunso* suggested that we ought to try and catch a few yaks for our own use. I agreed and we formed a party of three, the *gunso* and two POWs. The *gunso* would hold the guards and the men herding the cattle in conversation and we would rustle one or two yaks. Sometimes the herd was stretched out over such a large distance that there was no need for the *gunso* to hold the guards and herdsmen in conversation and we could steal two or three yaks without being noticed.

The yaks had to be hidden from prying eyes, so we took them into the jungle where they had plenty to eat. When they arrived at our camp they were very thin from being driven a long distance from the coastal plain. Hiding them in the jungle gave them a chance to fatten up.

As soon as we had four or five fattened up we killed and ate the first one. The meal – with the first meat we had eaten for a year and a half – was delicious. Naturally we had to bribe the guards with the best parts of the carcass, but the rest of the meat was excellent.

The guards were enjoying the meat as much as we were, and so they kept the rustling secret; we built up a herd which reached fifteen. One yak, a cow with only one horn, was the leader of the herd, and the *gunso* managed to get a bell to tie on her. She kept the herd together and we could hear the bell when she was wandering in the jungle, to locate it. The jungle in the hill above the camp was not thick, more like an English wood, so locating the yak was not too difficult. After killing and eating an animal the remains had to be carefully buried so that no one would suspect we were getting meat.

We were lucky that our camp appeared to have been forgotten by the Japanese, since nobody came to inspect us and thus discover a yak being cooked. The meat in the diet gave the men renewed vigour and no doubt helped many to survive their further experiences in Thailand.

When herding the cattle we explored the jungle. There was a stream which flowed down to the River Kwai and the water in it was crystal clear.

Those herding the cattle would bathe in this stream as we thought it was safe from infection. It came straight out of the jungle and flowed down from the hill with no habitation near it and no possibility of contamination from human beings.

At that stage of our captivity we had not heard of leptospirosis, called Japanese river fever in Malaya. It is a disease spread by rats' urine, and before the discovery of antibiotics, was usually fatal. There are plenty of rats in the jungle and it was probable that most rivers and streams would be contaminated with the spirochaetes of leptospirosis. Luckily we did not know about leptospirosis and, in our ignorance, bathed happily.

Keeping still while tending the herd of yaks so as not to disturb them feeding, we observed many jungle creatures. The most fantastic were the lizards, creatures about a foot long, with the most vivid green and red coloration I have ever seen. They had crests along their backs and looked like small prehistoric dinosaurs. Basking in the sun they could be observed lying on the many limestone rock outcrops in the jungle.

There was the odd snake to be seen, but lizards were in the majority. There may have been larger animals, but animals such as the big cats do not hunt in the daytime, and we were always back in camp well before dusk. The smaller animals, such as rats, were rarely sighted.

One day some high ranking Japanese officers came to visit the camps and the railway. The *gunso* was very busy with them and one evening explained to me that they wanted to make some purchases from the Thai traders.

The next day I duly assembled the traders and we met the Japanese officers. We sat in the shape of the letter U, with the Japanese sitting tailor fashion down one side of the U and the Thai traders squatting, facing them on the other side of the U. The *gunso* sat by the Japanese officers and I sat by the Thais to complete the letter U.

The Japanese would make a request which the *gunso* translated into Malay to me and then I translated the Malay into Thai for the traders. The answer went back in the reverse direction in all three languages – a laborious business. The officers were wanting fruit and other things that the Thais could supply, so the whole proceedings passed off satisfactorily; the Thais traded without too much haggling over price.

The Japanese were obviously pleased and complimented the *gunso*. He in turn showed us his appreciation with some extra gifts that night. It was a strange experience and could have gone badly wrong because the Thais were not over fond of the Japanese.

The advent of the high ranking officers puzzled us for a while but the reason for the visit soon came clear. They were obviously considering the state of progress of the railway and had decided that it was now complete up to Tonchan.

Although their presence could be explained by this decision it did not explain their wish to buy goods from the Thai traders at our particular camp. As far as I knew, they would have had as much success at any one of the other local camps.

Looking at the episode in hindsight, perhaps word had filtered through to the higher echelons in Bangkok that Tonchan South was a well organized camp, with trading facilities. The reputation of the *gunso* for maintaining a trouble-free camp could also have been part of the information. This aspect of the visit may have been nearer the truth than I thought, because, at a later date, when I met Oburi again, he had been promoted.

There was no doubt that Oburi *gunso* had given considerable help to all POWs in Tonchan South. The improvement in rations, mainly due to getting meat, the treatment of skin complaints, and the lessening of interference from the guards, had all contributed to improving the troops' spirits, and thus helped them to survive the hazards of POW life.

The camps at Tonchan we learnt were only temporary, and were to be dismantled when this section of the railway was considered finished; they were the only temporary sites.

The decision was now taken that the section was finished and we were given orders to move on up country, having dismantled the camp.

# CHAPTER IX

# A slow boat to Burma

The camp at Tonchan South was now closed down. The tents and camp equipment were taken down to the river and loaded by stages on to a barge, until little remained. The *gunso* told me to go with the barge and take one other POW. I chose a Dutchman who had come from Java; I thought he would be useful up country to sort out any problems, being better acquainted with jungle conditions than I was. Of mixed Javanese and Dutch descent, he had been a minor government official in Java. Having also been a sergeant in an infantry regiment he proved himself of great use on the barge.

The orders from the Japanese headquarters were that the *gunso* would march up the road from camp to camp and the barge would go up the river, meeting the road party at each camp. The barge was towed by a small launch in which were four guards with orders where they had to report. It was loaded with rations for the road party as well as with the tents and equipment.

The barge was large, about fifty feet long by ten or so feet wide and built of teak – a good solid construction. At the stern was a platform for the steersman to hold the rudder to guide the towed barge. Above this platform was a wooden canopy, providing shade for the steersman.

Just in front of the platform was a hatch-way down to a cabin with a semicircular roof. In this cabin lived the Thai barge owner and his family, consisting of his wife and two small children. In front of this cabin, the semi circular roof was continued to cover a hold in which were the stores.

The roof did not reach to the sides of the barge; a narrow gangway allowed passage from the stern to the bows of the boat. This gangway was about one foot wide, and there were no hand-holds on the roof, so it needed a steady foothold.

Entrance to the hold was at the front of the barge and from floor boards to the roof in the middle of the hold was about six feet. The bows had a triangular platform from which one stepped down into the hold; all the loading of the barge took place from this platform.

On the front platform was a post to which was tied the rope for towing, and just behind the post was a small hatch from which it was possible to get into the forepeak of the boat and inspect the bows. At the front of the back platform – just behind the entrance to the family cabin – was a baulk of timber, part of the deck, that projected over the sides of the boat. On each side was a shallow hole into which the cooking equipment for the barge was put.

These cooking utensils consisted of a circular earthenware vessel with a space underneath for a charcoal fire and above this a pot with a lid – all one piece of pottery. The space for the fire had a hole at one point of its circumference. When the barge was moving this hole was pointing backwards, but the vessel could be turned to face the bows and thus increase the draught from the wind to fan the fire.

All the meals were cooked in two pots, one on each side of the barge. One pot held rice and the other the main part of the meal. Food could be fried or boiled in the pots in the way described for making a *bah mee* when we were at Tarsao. The pots were also used to boil water for washing, so that both the Thais and ourselves could wash in clean water.

The barge has been described in some detail because we were going to live on it for a long trip, which lasted for ten or more days. It was also of interest because many Thai families live in this way on boats on the numerous rivers and *klongs** in the country.

The launch used by the guards was an interesting adaptation of river craft. It consisted of three sections: a bow section, an oblong section, and an engine and steering section, all made of steel. The sides of all sections were of the same height; each was complete in itself and would float unaided.

The three sections were bolted together to form the launch. Other launches could be made by adding one or more oblong sections, so craft of different sizes could be made for any particular purpose. The only essential was that each had to have a bow and an engine section.

We were now ready to start our journey from Tonchan South, and set off late in the morning, at the same time as the road party started to march up country I did not envy them as I was bound for a much more leisurely journey. We had no idea how far they were going to march because we had no knowledge of our destination.

The tide was fairly strong so the speed of towing was slow. We tied up for the night and the Thai family cooked the first meal and ate it with us; it was a pleasant change from camp cooking. Our rations included Number 1 fish, which the Thais had dried in the sun as we moved up river. This was turned into a mixture with vegetables and rice, flavoured with onions, garlic and other herbs. Like the Thais we ate with our fingers from a small bowl and drank the liquid portion of the meal.

There was nothing for the Dutchman and me to do as we progressed up the river, other than to sit up in the bows and watch the countryside go by. We

---

* A *klong* can best be described as a canal running through settled areas as well as countryside.

had three meals a day, morning, noon and evening, all cooked by the barge owner's wife. Travelling in this leisurely way we reached our first port of call at Hin Tok and waited for the road party to catch us up.

We were not allowed off and a fatigue party from the road contingent came to collect rations from the barge. When the road party set off next day we moved off at the same time. It was obvious that we were going to be much quicker than those who were marching, and this proved to be the case at each stop.

The guards were also enjoying their relaxation from normal duties. Some of them tried fishing from their launch, although I did not see them catch anything. They had their own rations and were not dependent on the barge for food. After two or three days they had relaxed enough to give us their rifles for cleaning – although they wisely kept the ammunition on the launch. Apart from an occasional command, we hardly communicated with the guards.

We put in at various camps as we continued our trip up river, for many of which we did not find out the name. At each stop we saw Thai trading barges, obviously doing a roaring trade with the camp guards and probably the POWs too. Some of the camps had many barges, so there must have been large contingents of guards and prisoners.

Both we and the Thai family traded with the barges for food. Here the Dutch sergeant proved invaluable as he knew the local produce and other types of food. The Thais are fond of fermented shellfish products, such as powdered prawns dried in the sun and buried in sand for a few months to enhance the flavour.

Such specialities I enjoyed when fried – but boiled and added to a noodle dish, I found them hard to stomach. So the Dutch sergeant watched over the purchases from the traders and selected the types of food that Europeans liked. This allowed me to enjoy all the meals on the barge. By this time we no longer saw our own troops coming to the barge to collect rations. We tried to inquire where they were, but received no answer.

We put in at one camp where there was a large cantilever bridge. There we stayed for some time and I managed to talk to the POWs who came to the barge to collect stores.

The place, I think, was called Tamaran Park – probably the anglicisation of the Thai name, Tamarkan. I gathered that there had been an officers' working party at this camp who had disagreed with the Japanese engineers on the way to build the bridge. Somehow the British officers had persuaded the Japanese to let them take over the planning and building but when the bridge was near completion it had collapsed, and the Japanese had had to erect it again. The bridge had been nicknamed Shoko's Folly, *shoko* being the Japanese for officer. When, later on, I travelled by rail back down the river route, I remembered Shoko's Folly, and hoped the bridges over which we went had been made secure.

Some of the camps were right down by the river. Others that we could not see were higher up, depending on the actual route of the railway. The huts in all these camps were made of bamboo sides with palm leaf thatch, and some looked in good condition, while others looked in poor shape.

Each camp was responsible for building a section of the railway, and when their task was completed the rail-laying company came through – as it did at Tonchan – to lay the rails on the embankments built by the POWs. The section at Tonchan must have been an easier section than elsewhere; the camps in that area were not permanent as were the camps we were now visiting.

Half way up the river we picked up an Australian soldier, who was put on the boat without any explanation. This caused trouble with the Thai family. The Dutch sergeant and I had followed the custom of Thailand and did not wear shoes or any kind of footwear on the barge. It is usual in Asia, at least the tropical parts of it, to take off one's shoes when entering a house or any other kind of living accommodation. This ensures that no dirt contaminates the house and keeps down the incidence of disease. All floors are spotlessly clean and wearing one's shoes would make a person feel guilty of sullying the domestic conditions. The floors are often made of polished teak, in all but the poorest homes, and are polished until they shine. Walking on them with dirty shoes quickly ruins the beautiful surface.

The barge was kept immaculate by the barge owner; while he was cleaning the barge his wife was steering. The boards of the deck were swept and polished every day, so it was annoying to see the Australian refusing to remove his shoes. He said he was not going to behave like any bloody Boong – so the Dutch sergeant and I had to remove his shoes forcibly.

On questioning him I found out that that he had not washed for several months because cholera had stopped all washing unless boiled water could be obtained. I believed him; he stank and his skin was covered in small pustules. He was a very unprepossessing sight.

I banned him from coming aft to meet the Thai family because they obviously did not like him at all. In this I was grateful for the presence of the Dutch sergeant, a man who looked as if he would brook no trouble.

The peace of the barge's voyage had now been broken, as I had to watch out for friction between the Thais and the Australian. This was a pity because the voyage was proving very interesting. Few Europeans had probably made such a voyage and I was fascinated by the river traffic and the different aspects of the country through which we were passing.

The whole trip up the river was about one hundred and fifty miles – which accounts for the road party not keeping up with the barge. A march of this length under tropical conditions, with poor food, was weeding out those who were unfit. We presumed that those who fell sick were left behind at the various camps on the route.

After more than one week of working our way up river the Thai boatman started to look worried and was continually examining the bows of the barge. Although we made slow progress in distance travelled, the river was flowing quite fast so the pressure of water on the bows was more than he anticipated.

One morning he called me to look at the timbers on the bow, and made a remark. My Thai did not extend to nautical terms and it took some time to realize that he was worried about a crack in the bows. On closer examination we found there was a leak, which had to be repaired before it became worse. We tried to get the launch either to slow down or to stop, but the Japanese took no notice.

The boatman and I started to plug the leak between the planks by caulking with cotton cloth and some form of glue that he had. After working for most of the day he seemed satisfied, but wanted my opinion – not that I knew much about stopping leaks on barges. He pointed to the plugged leak and asked 'OK?' As far as I could see the crack was plugged so I answered 'OK!' He shook his head and repeated the question and I repeated my answer. The boatman then became irritated and said in response to my answer 'Mài, mài OK? mái'. Translated this is 'No, No, is it OK?' I replied again that it was OK, and we repeated this question and answer twice more.

I suddenly realized what was the trouble. His query contained OK on a rising tone, which to me was a question. I had replied with OK in a dropped tone, indicating to me that it was indeed OK. But the boatman did not recognize OK in a dropped tone; to him it was a completely different word from OK in a rising tone. So I tried a new technique and said 'Dài, dài OK?' Dài means good, so I was trying to say 'very good it's OK'. This succeeded and the boatman was relieved that I had at last understood and agreed with him that the leak had been cured.

Not long after this episode we pulled in to another camp and for some unknown reason the Australian was taken off the barge – to our great relief.

The river was now becoming narrower and shallower, so we were getting nearly as far as we could go by barge. Sure enough at the end of the day we pulled in to a camp perched on a bank above the river. It did not look a very pleasant camp and we hoped it was not the end of the trip – but it was. We had arrived at Nikki, the last camp on the railway before Three Pagoda Pass, the boundary between Burma and Thailand. It was just over ten miles or so from the camp to the boundary. The railway had been built from Moulmein in Burma to the pass and was joining up with the Thai side of the track.

The barge was unloaded by a working party and we looked out for the *gunso* and the rest of our party from Tonchan, but we could not find anyone we recognized. Where they had gone and why they did not reach Nikki was a mystery. The Dutch sergeant and I were put into the camp to join the others working there.

# CHAPTER X

# The golden nail

The accommodation at Nikki into which I was sent consisted of old, torn Indian Army tents. My particular tent was the outer cover of a tent and had several tears in the canvas through which the rain came. Inside the tent were two *changs*, one on each side, about three feet off the ground. When it rained – as it seemed to do every day – the ground was muddy and water sometimes flowed through the tent, so the *changs* were necessary to allow us to sleep.

Insufficient accommodation had been provided for all the men in the camp and we were crowded into the tents, with each person having about eighteen inches of *chang* on which to sleep. It was impossible to lie on your back as there was not enough room, so you had to lie on your side. We slept alternately head to foot so your head was between two pairs of feet. Before going to sleep you had to decide which was the least dirty pair of feet and then face those feet while trying to get to sleep.

The camp did have some spare clothes so once again I had a shirt and shorts with a pair of Japanese army boots – the ones with the space for the big toe and rubber soles with canvas uppers. We needed new clothes because we were wet through most days from rain. Nikki was way up in the mountains dividing Burma from Thailand, at a height of about three thousand feet. This made the climate quite cold at night and not too warm by day. The weather was cloudy and we experienced a shower of rain practically every day, with sometimes very heavy downpours.

The food had also deteriorated and once again the rations consisted of Number 2 fish and gascape stew. There was plenty of rice, but with such an unappetizing meal to accompany the rice nobody was tempted to eat a lot. Meals were provided first thing in the morning and last thing at night before we went to sleep.

The men in the camp were a mixed bunch. They were the remnants of the different forces sent up to Thailand and contained people from officers' working parties and also Asian labourers. The officers' working parties were almost entirely made up of Indian Army officers.

When the Japanese had told us about rest camps in the hills, parties of officers had been formed to enjoy the delights of relaxation in these camps.

On arrival in Thailand the officers found that they had to work to get their rations. From discussion it seemed that everybody had come from either P or H Forces and we formed the last 400 fit persons from these forces. The Asian labourers had been added to make up the numbers.

The camp at Nikki was formed for the last final spurt to get the railway completed on schedule, so all work was carried out with commands of 'speedo speedo'. The camp was organized on Tokyo time as before, so we rose in the dark, had breakfast in the dark and moved off at sunrise, some times just day-light with rain when the sun was not visible. On a normal day we returned to camp to have one and a half hour's daylight before dark.

I was allotted to a working party of four men, with the same guard every day. The party consisted of an Australian officer, one private from an infantry regiment, a Dutchman and me. Our job was felling trees, and we were issued with an axe and a cross-cut saw.

Off we set from camp and climbed up slippery paths into the surrounding hilly country. Some of the paths were very steep and you always prayed that it was not your turn to carry the cross-cut saw when climbing up these paths. Balancing a large saw on your shoulder requires a degree of agility if you are not going to slip and cut yourself.

Our daily task was to fell six trees, each ten metres tall without branches – and these were big trees. We started cutting on one side with the cross-cut saw and chopping with the axe on the opposite side. The axe cut a V-shaped notch and this caused the tree to bend over slightly, otherwise the saw became stuck in the cut.

Our team was lucky in having the Australian officer, who had worked as a backwoodsman in Australia. He taught us how to fell trees and undoubtedly saved us a lot of unnecessary extra labour. When the trees had been felled they were collected by elephants and carried off to a sawmill.

Felling the trees in this hilly country was an art, and here the Australian was again most useful. He would argue with the guard as to which direction the tree should fall after felling. Once or twice we were unlucky and having felled the tree we watched it go bouncing down the steep hillside right into the river, a good three hundred feet below us.

When felling on a slope it was difficult to get a firm foothold to swing the axe or to pull on the saw. We took it in turns to use the tools, with a rota-tion of saw – axe – rest – saw. This gave one man a rest while the other three worked. The rest was necessary as no food was supplied during the day and hence there was no rest period for the whole party.

After a day felling trees everybody was certainly ready for a rest at night. The work went on seven days a week with no respite, in order to get the rail-way finished. When a tree had been felled the trunk had to be cut just below the first branch. The tree was usually lying on the ground, caught up in the branches of other trees; the skill was to fell it so that it was as clear as possible and yet would not roll down the hill to the river. Cutting off a trunk under these conditions was no easy task and often took longer than the actual felling. If we lost a tree we still had to make our quota of six trees, so some days we were late back to camp, and lost our period of rest before sunset.

While working on tree felling I cut my index finger and after a while it festered. Sick parade was after our return to camp so I had to work all day before reporting sick. There was only one doctor, a Hollander, in the camp. He said he would have to lance my finger and then bind it up. No anaesthetic was available, so two orderlies held my hand rigid while the wound was lanced and cleaned.

It was then bound up and I was officially declared fit for medicine and duty so off to work the next day with the bound finger. The other members of the team helped as much as possible to shield me from opening the wound, and it gradually healed. With the cooler climate there was less chance of any infection taking hold.

The Japanese decided that they had almost enough trees cut down to make the final bridge over a small tributary of the River Kwai. The four of us were taken off tree felling and I was posted to a pile-driving team. This was just as well because my clothing was wearing out. The work in the jungle had torn the clothes and the rain had helped them to disintegrate, so I had a very ragged appearance. Most of the POWs were in the same state.

The pile driving was purely manual. A bamboo framework in the shape of a triangular arch was erected where the log had to be driven into the ground. This framework had cross pieces to strengthen it and provide a means of climbing it. The whole contraption was about twelve metres tall and was held by ropes, acting as stays.

The bamboo framework was suitably placed by the engineers and then the log to be used as a pile was dragged up in place by the framework. A long iron rod with a pointed end was set vertically in the middle of the top of the log and aligned with it. The rod carried a heavy weight which could slide up and down.

This weight was attached to ropes running over a pulley at the top of the bamboo framework and leading to a wooden spar. This spar had twelve ropes tied to it so that when the ropes were pulled the spar raised the weight. The twelve ropes, inclined at a steep angle from the men to the wooden spar, were pulled by twelve men standing on the ground about twenty feet from the bamboo framework.

A Japanese engineer sat on the top of the framework and sang out the time, which we repeated. The engineer waved his hands to beat out the time, rather like the conductor of an orchestra, but without the baton. The refrain was: '*Ichi ni no san yo, no san yo, no san yo, no san YO*' – the Japanese for 'one two and three four, and three four and three four and three FOUR'. At each word each man pulled in the rope hand over hand, and on the last word suddenly let go, but still holding the rope end. Pulling the ropes had raised the heavy weight and when we let go it descended rapidly and drove the pile into the ground.

If you forgot, or had become lazy, and did not let go of your rope, you were dragged over the ground. People soon learnt to handle their ropes properly and pile driving proceeded apace. The POWs working on the job were a very mixed collection. I had an NCO from the Air Force on my left and a Tamil labourer on my right, and we usually kept the same places in our team of twelve.

We began first thing in the morning and continued throughout the day, irrespective of whether the sun shone or it poured with rain. I do not remember whether there was a fixed task of a certain number of piles to be driven, but we could finish only when the last pile was driven home to the engineer's satisfaction.

There was no rest for food, the only respite from pile driving being the moving of the framework and the erecting of the next log. The piles were being driven in to form a bridge over a small stream, and horizontal pieces were put on as soon as there were two uprights.

The work was being carried out as fast as possible, so it was essential that as many POWs as possible were available for work. To ensure a maximum turnout, the Japanese limited the number of sick in hospital to ten per cent of the total in the camp. As we had 400 men, the hospital sick list was therefore limited to forty men.

After some time working in the pile driving team I developed amoebic dysentery again, so one evening I reported sick to the Hollander doctor. He confirmed I had dysentery and suspected the amoebic variety. However he could not admit me to hospital because there were people already in the hospital who were more ill than I was. So I had to go back to work – not happily, because hauling on the rope did not do my dysentery much good.

After a couple of days I reported sick again and the doctor said 'How many stools a day?' I replied 'twenty-eight' thinking this would give me a good chance of getting into hospital, but I was not even put on the waiting list. Another day or two and back I went and the same question was asked. This time I replied 'thirty-two' and he asked me how I knew.

The counting was easy. One of the men had died and I inherited a book from him; it was a rather tatty copy of Rob Roy by Sir Walter Scott. Although still using the bottle each time I went to the lavatory I also used one-quarter of a page of Rob Roy so eight pages a day were being used. The doctor thought this was getting serious and, at last, placed me on the waiting list. But this did not prevent me from going out pile driving.

Finally I went to report sick again and reported forty-two stools a day I said if it was not treated soon I would overtake myself reading Rob Roy.

The doctor decided this was serious enough for me to be admitted to hospital. In order to do so one patient had to be discharged – the limit of forty could not be exceeded.

Although several people had died so we no longer had four hundred in our camp, the Japanese still allowed forty sick people in hospital. When I entered I was practically skin and bone and most of my workmates thought I was due for the boneyard, as the cemetery was affectionately known. I lay on the *chang* in the hospital tent gradually becoming weaker because the food was repulsive and I could not eat to keep up my strength. Meanwhile the doctor was giving me what few drugs he possessed.

I had inherited a dead man's book and now I had inherited a dead man's bed. The patient who was going to be ejected to make way for me was saved because a man had died. I was in this state of slowly becoming weaker when my luck changed.

One day the *gunso* from Tonchan South camp came visiting the sick. He had been promoted and he now wore a short sword, showing he was a sergeant major. He saw me lying on my *chang* and came over to speak to me. He asked me why I was in the hospital and I told him I had dysentery, not being able to distinguish between the two varieties either in Malay or Japanese. I said I was not improving because I could not eat the hospital food. He nodded, wished me well and left the tent.

That I thought, was it, but not so. That evening the *gunso* returned, bringing with him his own food. He gave me this and took mine away; whether he ate it or threw it away I did not know. He came for two days, bringing his food and taking mine. The better food improved my condition and the drugs supplied by the doctor started to work, and I slowly recovered.

I had lost so much weight that I was down to just over five stone and looked like a scarecrow. As I was getting better and the other inmates of the hospital had ulcers and malaria I was deemed fitter than them. Consequently I was put on hospital fatigues, because nobody could be spared from the working parties to look after the hospital. My job was working in the cookhouse – which seemed strange since I was suffering from an enteric complaint.

I think that without the food supplied by Oburi *gunso*, I probably would have died from sheer exhaustion from the effects of the dysentery – in which case, I can regard Oburi's action as having saved my life. The effects of the good food in Tonchan South was also a contributing factor, together with not being exhausted by having to march up to the Burmese border. These contributing factors, I also owed, if indirectly, to Oburi.

The effect of the 'speedo' managed to get the railway route finished and the line laying company came through and completed the line. Work was now reduced to tidying up the railway and we heard there was going to be a grand ceremony to celebrate the completion of the line.

A CUTTING – BURMA-SIAM RAILWAY. After blasting the rock face and breaking up the lumps that were too heavy to move, the prisoners were formed into an endless human chain. Then, basketful by basketful, they hauled the tons of rubble to the edge of the cutting and tipped it into the valley below. This routine could continue for as long as sixteen hours. By Ronald Searle (RS)

THE SELERANG BARRACKS INCIDENT. Seventeen thousand prisoners were imprisoned in three barrack blocks until they agreed to sign a document promising not to try to escape. Latrines were dug in the tarmac parade ground and soon disease – including diphtheria – began to spread amongst prisoners. After a few days it was agreed to sign the documents, emphasising that this was done under duress. See page 18.
By Philip Meninsky (PM)

Ronald Searle

Street Scene, Singapore 1942.    Heads of executed Malay 'underground' workers exhibited as a warning by Japs

STREET SCENE, SINGAPORE. The Japanese used to display the heads of people executed, by beheading, on planks on the roundabouts 'pour discourager les autres'. (RS)

A STOP AND A CHANCE TO WASH. We had not had a wash since leaving Singapore so when the train stopped those in trucks near the engine dashed to the water supply for the engine. At every major station there was a large tank with an arm that swung out, carrying a hose pipe. See page 37. (PM)

THE UBIQUITOUS BAMBOO. The roofs of our huts were made of *atap*, a type of bamboo with narrow leaves. Along each wall was a low platform of bamboo called a *chang*, about six inches high. See page 39. (PM)

THE MARCH TO TARSAO. Part of the journey was through jungle, along a muddy track which had been churned up by lorries. Prisoners and guards were wearied and stretched out over quite a distance. All semblance of an organised march had disappeared. See page 43. (PM)

CAMP IN THE JUNGLE. Monsoon tropical jungle is not as thick as tropical rain forest jungle, but it took us three days to clear enough space for a tented camp. The tall trees gave it an eerie appearance; lianas hung from the trees and the sunlight was greatly reduced in the shade. It was not unlike a dim cathedral See page 44. (PM).

WORK PARADE. The Japanese engineers decided what work would be carried out each day and how many men they thought were necessary to perform the tasks. The parties had to be balanced against the number of men required for camp fatigues and also the number of sick, both those hospitalised and those fit for medicine and duty. (RS)

Ronald Searle

Cholera lines. - Thai-Burma Railway.

Cholera waves reduced the populations
of the slave camps to 50% in a few
weeks.

THE CHOLERA LINES – BURMA RAILWAY. This drawing was made at Tarsao camp; the man in the foreground was, like the author, one of the lucky survivors. Cholera reduced the populations of some camps by 50 per cent in four weeks. See page 64. (RS)

THE OPERATING THEATRE. Operations were performed in primitive conditions in a bamboo and *atap* hut. Most of the instruments had been made in the camp and the supply of general anaesthetics was limited. The operation in the drawing was an emergency appendicectomy. Note that the patient's eyes are covered, as in this case he is fully awake. See page 107. (PM)

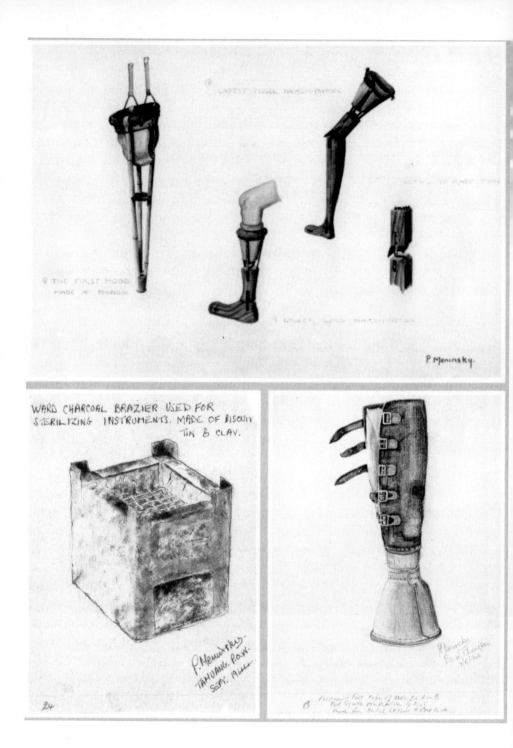

IMPROVISED MEDICAL EQUIPMENT. There were highly skilled technicians amongst the POWs and they created some amazing and vital pieces of equipment, including artificial limbs. (PM)

CHANGI GAOL, SINGAPORE. A grim, sinister place that nearly broke the spirits of many of the prisoners. (RS)

THE WONDERFUL NEWS. On the day that the Japanese surrendered a Thai family came to break the news to Philip Meninsky and his fellow prisoner in the cemetery at Nakom Paton. (PM)

*Changi Aug. 31 1945*
*Ronald Searle*

*First Parachute supplies dropping near Changi Gaol*

FIRST PARACHUTE SUPPLIES DROPPING NEAR CHANGI GAOL, bringing
much needed food. It was necessary to heed the warning not to overeat – or smoke – after
years of a meagre diet. (RS)

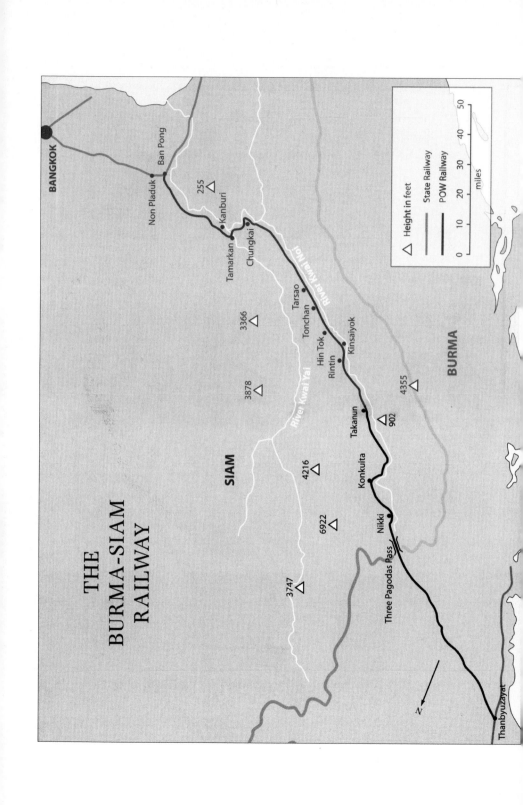

# THE
# BURMA-SIAM
# RAILWAY

BANGKOK

Non Pladuk
Ban Pong

Kanburi
255 △

Tamarkan
Chungkai

River Kwai Noi

Tarsao
Tonchan
3366 △

Hin Tok
Rintin
Kinsaiyok

3878 △

River Kwai Yai

SIAM

Takanun
4355 △
902 △

Konkuita

4216 △

Nikki

6922 △

Three Pagodas Pass

3747 △

BURMA

N

Thanbyuzayat

△ Height in feet
— State Railway
— POW Railway

0   10   20   30   40   50
miles

I do not think any POW saw the ceremony but we heard about it; it was the hammering in of a golden nail to mark the completion of the track. This ceremony took place somewhere near Konkuite and on the Thai side of the Three Pagoda Pass. There was great rejoicing amongst the Japanese troops but no celebratory gifts came the way of the POW camp. We just soldiered on as usual.

There was some joy, however, as the Japanese decided to evacuate the worst sick from the camp and send them down to the base camps. The doctor was told to parade all his sick from the hospital so that a Japanese doctor could decide who would be evacuated.

One morning the patients were told to pack up their belongings and parade down near the river. We did so and a Japanese came round to inspect us. I did not fancy my chances of evacuation because a person suffering from amoebic dysentery does not look very ill. The patients with ulcers were obviously prime candidates because their illness was very visible.

Those suffering from malaria could, with any luck, display a good rigor, and, in any case, usually had a temperature. Enteric complaints were not that visible. When the doctor inspected me he asked the Hollander doctor what was the matter, and he was told I had dysentery. I was then put on the waiting list, but had to compete with the others also suffering from such complaints.

The original plan was to send only the hospital patients, but the damp had added several more to the hospital quota, making a total of seventy-five. The Japanese discussed the situation and in the end decided to send sixty sick down to the base camps.

On parade in the sun the weaker members began to fall down. Everybody waited in anticipation of whether they would stand a chance of survival down the river or whether they would die in Nikki. At last the people for evacuation were chosen and to my relief I was among them. We were told to pick up our belongings and to march down to the river's edge. Even the sick rallied in their eagerness to make the river transport.

We found a sampan waiting for us and everyone climbed aboard in haste before the Japanese changed their minds. I wondered whether the *gunso* had helped in arranging the evacuation of the POWs and also whether he had been instrumental in allowing sixty – and not just forty – men to be sent to the base camps. It was noticeable that no Asian labourers were included.

If it were the *gunso* who had helped in these decisions, then I, and the few survivors from our trip south, owed him a lot. I doubt whether I would have made the original forty.

We were overjoyed as we sat in the sampan; we had escaped from Nikki.

# CHAPTER XI

# On the road to Kanburi

The sixty sick men boarded the sampan with some difficulty, being weak from illness and waiting on parade for such a long time. The boat was about fifty feet long with a semicircular cover of woven palm leaves extending for most of its length. There was a small platform at both the stern and the bows. The cover extended to the sides of the sampan, so that there was no gangway; to get from stern to bows, you had to pass under the cover. The hold was the space under this palm leaf cover. The steersman sat at the stern with a rudder, and a rope was fastened to a post on the platform at the bows for towing by a launch.

The men were lying on empty rice sacks on the floor of the hold, resting after the trials of getting on board. When we finally cast off and started down river there was a sigh of relief from everyone. It looked as if life was getting easier and all we had to do was to lie on the sacks and rest for the trip down river.

The sampan stopped late in the afternoon at a camp with POWs in huts. We were ordered off the boat with our belongings and marched up to one of the huts which was empty and had *changs*. It was a typical POW hut with bamboo sides and a palm thatch roof.

We all waited hopefully for some food but none appeared. Our three guards were nowhere to be seen and no POW members of the camp came to see us. We finally went to sleep, there being nothing else to do, but were woken up Tokyo time when it was still dark. No food was offered, instead the guards ordered us out on parade. There we were checked and some guards from the camp came to inspect us.

When the sun rose at daybreak we were told to march off, still having had no food. We walked rather than marched – and after a short while we stumbled rather than walked – along the road, continually encouraged by the guards to keep together. Periodically a halt was called and stragglers joined us again. No sooner had they all joined the party than off we set again.

Some of the party were now becoming very ill and those with leg ulcers were having great trouble in keeping up with the main body of the party. Eventually the guards began to halt at regular intervals because they too needed a rest, but now they did not wait for any stragglers. Presumably the stragglers just gave up the impossible struggle and lay down by the side of the road and died.

When we halted we had noticed that we had lost some members of the party. But as we were such a mixed lot, from so many different groups of troops, nobody knew anybody else so checking was not readily possible. We marched all day and late in the afternoon came to another hutted camp with POWs. A hut was made available for us and we sank on to the *changs*, grateful for the respite.

The guards had disappeared, as usual, and we were getting the impression that nobody on the route knew why we were coming or when we were coming; certainly they displayed no interest in us. When we had recovered we managed to speak to some of the POWs from the camp and told them we had had nothing to eat for two days. They responded and managed to produce some food after night had fallen.

The food was very welcome and we ate a reasonable meal and went to sleep feeling better. Next morning we marched to a station and waited for a train. It was composed of four or five rice trucks – the same as those we had travelled up in from Singapore – and was pulled by one of the adapted lorries. We climbed into the rice trucks, with between ten and fifteen men in a truck, so conditions were not overcrowded.

The train eventually started and we set off down the line towards the base camps. The journey was not smooth because the train kept stopping and starting again and, when stationary, the trucks became very hot. Some of the men were now in a bad way, and were becoming unconscious. By the early afternoon two in our truck had died.

We kept them in the truck but within a short time in came the flies and the bodies started to smell. After a short discussion it was decided that they would have to be thrown on to the side of the track; this we reluctantly did. We did not know who they were of where they came from, only that one was English and one was Dutch.

The train stopped finally early in the afternoon and everyone was ordered off. We paraded as well as we could and then marched off to a nearby camp. Once again it was one of the permanent camps with huts and we were put into an empty hut. This time we did not manage to contact any of the men in the camp, so went hungry to bed on the *changs*. We feared there would be no food in the morning and we were right – there wasn't.

We paraded at dawn and set off, leaving some men behind. These were mainly the cases with leg ulcers who had given up the unequal struggle of marching with legs that were almost useless.

This was a short march, only about two to three hours, with the guards giving us the usual rest periods, but some of the men dropped out by the wayside and died if no one saw them. It was not very probable that they would be seen lying by the road because between camps the road was practically deserted.

We arrived at a station and waited there for a train, consisting of the usual rice trucks and lorry engine. We scrambled aboard the trucks and set off with the train starting and stopping as before. In the early afternoon we went round an escarpment, with the track going over a viaduct which clung to the cliff face. The train rattled and swayed and we hoped that the structure would hold until we reached the other end. We had heard tales of just how rickety the viaducts were and we had seen the ramshackle construction of some of the bridges which we had built. However, the viaduct held together and we were back on solid ground with the jungle on both sides of the track.

The train pulled into a station and we descended and paraded, before marching off to another permanent camp. This consisted of the usual collection of dilapidated huts and we were once again put into an empty hut. Fortunately we managed to contact some of the troops billeted in the camp and they provided a welcome meal; by this time we were literally starving.

The progress of the journey so far implied that the camps did not know we were due to arrive, and that our guards did not carry much authority. They seemed to have been detailed to take a group of POWs down to the base camp, but were not responsible for delivering a definite number of sick personnel; we were not counted on our parades.

The next morning – after no breakfast as usual – we paraded and waited while the guards went off to arrange for the remainder of the journey. Eventually we went down to the river, still the Kwai, and embarked on a large rice barge, with a deep hold but completely uncovered.

Those who were very sick were lowered into the hold and the rest of us sat on the stern and bow platforms. We were towed by a small launch and set off for what was to become the final stage of our journey. An Indian Army captain and I started chatting; although we were hungry the rest was reviving us and we began to take an interest in the journey.

We passed a viaduct built round the face of a high cliff and wondered just how the POWs had managed to build such a structure; the cliff was almost vertical. We passed other camps and several Thai barges going upstream, and some anchored by the camps.

The pair of us must have looked an odd sight. The captain was covered in a sheet, wearing his army service cap with the cap badge of the Sikh regiment, and sporting a pair of *chaplis*, the Indian type of sandals, with overlapping uppers held by a strap round the ankle. I had my sarong, faithful trilby hat and a pair of Japanese boots.

The captain was very proud of his sheet. It had lasted without tearing and had been used for all purposes while he was in an officers' working party;

by night it was a sheet, and by day a sarong. It was made of a type of cotton called *mazri*, which is very hard wearing – the reason for which he had bought it in India.

His bearer, the Indian servant provided by the army, had poured scorn on the cloth, as Indian soldiers would not use *mazri*; they said it was worn and used only by the very poor and the outcasts. But the captain was determined that when he got back to India he would buy more and use it for sheets.

All the people on the barge were ragged, dirty, and unkempt because we had had no facilities for washing during the whole trip. We were looking forward to getting to a camp where we could wash and clean what few garments we possessed. Of the original sixty who had set out there were now seventeen survivors.

Those not with us had either died, been left behind in other camps, or even just forgotten, as there was no recognisable organization of the group. We had come over two hundred miles in five days and four nights, existing on two meals, with everybody classified as hospital cases or possible hospital cases.

In mid-afternoon we arrived at Kanchanaburi and disembarked. We were paraded in front of a camp and questioned as to the forces we belonged to. One or two may have been incorrectly classified because some did not know their Force; this was determined by where they had begun work in Thailand.

The sick were divided into two groups, one group of men belonging to F and H Forces, and a few belonging to other forces in the second group. Those belonging to F and H Forces were admitted into the camp, while the second group was sent off to another base camp at Chungkai, which was across the river.

Both Kanchanaburi and Chungkai were on the River Kwai. Kanchanaburi – the name was often shortened to Kanburi – was a walled town just up the road from the camp. This was surrounded by a five foot high wall of palm leaf mat, and when we arrived the members of the camp were looking over the wall to see if they recognized anybody.

We were led into the camp and given accommodation. The huts were of the usual type, made of bamboo walls with palm leaf thatch. Inside, there were two *changs*, one against each wall, and each of us was allotted a space on a *chang*.

Just as I had settled down, Robert, the other officer who had been with the company when we set off for Thailand from Singapore, appeared, carrying a four-gallon tin full of clean water. I was very grateful and thanked him; little did I know what a sacrifice he was making. He told me how to find him amongst all the huts, and said I could get a few clothes from a store in the camp.

Before attending to details of personal comfort I had to report to the doctor to ascertain from what disease I was suffering. I gave him a résumé of my complaint and he asked for a stool to test; this was provided at a later time – in a hollow bamboo stem. The camp had certain medical facilities, including the ability to make examinations of specimens by microscope.

The next day it was confirmed that I was suffering from amoebic dysentery.

The long journey without food had effected a partial cure as I was not as ill as I had been. I was put on a diet of tapioca. Breakfast was plain tapioca, lunch was tapioca with limes, cut up skin and all, and dinner was eggs boiled in tapioca. I enjoyed the bland diet and regained my strength, but was kept on the diet to prevent a recurrence of dysentery. The camp had a canteen and the usual items from the Thai traders were on sale. It was now that I found out just how good a friend Robert had been. Water was short in the camp and had to be purchased at three dollars a four-gallon tin. A person was allowed to buy only four gallons once a week, so Robert had gone without most of his week's supply.

The four gallons had to make do for all purposes, drinking and washing. Tea was supplied with the meals in fairly copious quantities, so washing was the main requisite. By the end of the week the water in the tin started to look like coffee, with heaps of grounds in the bottom. This, of course, was the dust washed off during the week.

The answers to a few questions now became clear. When up-country we had often wondered why we were called the Singapura Force, the term being applied to both F and H Forces. We learnt that Singapura is the Asian name for Singapore, used also by the Japanese.

F and H Forces together totalled ten thousand men and officers, and these troops had been lent by the commander of POWs in Singapore to the commander of POWs in Thailand. Apparently, the rank of the commanding Japanese officer depended on the number of POWs under his charge. By obtaining ten thousand POWs from the Singapore command the commander in Thailand had managed to be promoted to the next higher rank.

The POWs of the Singapura group were thus listed in both commands and both Japanese commanders enjoyed the higher rank. However, news percolated through to Singapore that the POWs of the Singapura forces were dying and that their numbers were decreasing. This alarmed the Singapore commander because he could see that his rank was in danger if the numbers fell too low.

Accordingly, Thailand was requested to send back the Singapura group, whose numbers had now fallen to almost five thousand. This request took some time to filter through the various chains of command but at last it did, and was the reason we had been evacuated to Kanburi, ready to be transported back to Singapore.

By the time we had all arrived back in Kanburi, the numbers had fallen even further, to just above four thousand, so orders were given by Singapore to provide better food and better medical facilities to keep us alive. This was the explanation for the big improvement in food, with occasionally some meat being provided as well. There were even special diets for the very sick – including my bland tapioca diet. As much pay as possible was made available to the other ranks and the officers continued to get their thirty yen a month. In addition, all men were given full rations, irrespective of whether they were sick or not. The Japanese command was making a big attempt to maintain the health of the POWs by providing good food and medical help.

To begin with the weather in Kanburi was fine with no rain and I had little to do other than eat, walk around the camp and chat with the various people I knew. My neighbour on my left on the *chang* was the Volunteer officer who had been cut by the bamboo we felled when we first arrived at Tonchan South.

His leg had been amputated about four months before and had healed well. He could move around on crutches but was still unsure of them because they were a very crude attempt at a walking aid. It was essential that he tried, particularly to go to the latrine, as otherwise he would have been dependent on the few hospital orderlies we had available.

On my right hand side was a Hollander officer who was in a bad way, with malaria and dysentery. He just lay on the *chang*, eating very little food and requiring a bamboo bedpan frequently. Each time he turned fleas jumped off his blankets. We were plagued with fleas and lice, because of the crowded conditions and lack of sufficient washing facilities. Every morning we sat outside the hut and picked off the lice, squashing them with our fingernails; my biggest count was one hundred and nineteen.

Somebody persuaded the Japanese to allow us to get to the baggage we had left at Non Pladuk and from there we took at least one piano. This was put in our hut and most nights we had community singing. An airforce sergeant who had been in a service band was a very good pianist and he would play all the popular tunes we remembered from before our capture. He also sang to his own accompaniment. This provided entertainment to keep up our spirits and was a help in overcoming sickness.

The camp needed working parties and these were a mixed bag, involving all ranks, as it gave an opportunity to get outside the camp and see the rest of the world. There was one delightful story of an Australian who was detailed for an unloading party down by the town. As he was carrying sacks of rice up from a barge he was approached by a Thai prostitute, who intimated, through sign language, that she had not experienced a European. To extend her knowledge of mankind she offered to take the Australian to bed in her hut in the village. This would have been quite possible, for there were no guards on these parties.

However, looking at the girl the Australian decided that she was definitely a health risk, and knowing the Japanese outlook on sexual matters, thought he should refuse. But how to do so without hurting the girl's feelings, as she had made such a generous offer? He decided the best excuse was lack of stamina and intimated he would love to accept but he was too weak from lack of meat.

The girl nodded wisely and moved off, leaving the Australian breathing a sigh of relief. To his surprise she returned after an hour bringing a juicy steak, accompanied by vegetables and some noodles. Here was temptation indeed, and what was he going to do? An anguished decision was made; with mouth watering he turned down the meal and the prostitute departed in a huff.

The weather hitherto had been fine with no rain, making the camp very dusty, but now storm clouds appeared and we began to experience heavy downpours instead of dust we had mud. But this was the least of our worries – the main problem was the camp latrines.

These were the usual trenches about ten feet deep and three feet wide, with the length depending on where they were sited. During the dry weather they had functioned perfectly well, with the contents draining into the nearby ground.

With the rains the latrines started to fill up with water and very soon the contents approached the top of the trench. The sewage was a seething mass of maggots, which did not cause us much concern during the dry weather because the level was a good five feet below the surface. But with the rains the maggots started to crawl out of the latrine and onto the three bamboo poles laid across the trench – on which we had to squat.

Going to the latrines was now extremely unpleasant because the maggots crawled over your feet as you squatted on the bamboo poles. Remembering that water was in short supply, eliminating the maggots from your feet became an unpleasant task. The rains also made the bamboo poles more slippery than they were before, so extra care was needed, especially at night, to negotiate a trip to the latrines. One or two of the weaker members of the camp actually fell into the sewage – a dreadful fate as cleaning up after such an accident was troublesome with the lack of water.

The horrors of those latrines stayed in everybody's minds for a long time and was one of the lasting impressions of the camp at Kanburi. The camp at Chungkai, on the other side of the River Kwai, was not near any human habitation, so the occupants had to come to Kanburi to get their stores for the canteen. One day I saw in the distance my friend who had started to teach me Thai, but he was too far away to talk to him. The troops were still being sorted out, so that only the members of the Singapura force were in Kanburi and all those from other forces were in Chungkai.

From the exchanges of men between the camps that were taking place we learnt about the camp in Chungkai. They also had medical facilities from the original K Force of medical personnel that had been sent to Thailand. Apparently conditions were about the same as in Kanburi. Those who became fit, however, were being sent back to the original camps up-country, where their work was to maintain the railway track.

The water shortage was beginning to produce skin complaints, the worst of which was scabies. Although the camp was reasonably well supplied with medicines there was a lack of suitable drugs for scabies – and we had no access to sulphur blocks as we had at Tonchan South. Those infected with the complaint had no immediate remedy and in many cases the scabies pimples became infected and the condition turned into septic scabies. The scabies, other skin infections, lice and fleas, produced a collection of people who were continually scratching; even after the period of captivity was over, an ex-POW from the East could always be recognized by his continual scratching.

Another complaint was called foot rot. This condition produced thick skin on the soles of the feet, with the skin roughened and crinkled like the hide of an elephant. There did not seem to be any cure, although eventually the skin healed when kept dry, so presumably it was caused by the feet constantly being wet when working in the camps during rainy weather.

Although Kanburi camp had medical officers and working parties, it was really one large hospital for the remnants of F and H Forces. By now there were no troops from other forces and the numbers stood at about three thousand eight hundred.

After the rains the weather turned cooler and for a while was pleasant. Then it became quite cold, probably dropping to about 65 degrees Fahrenheit. As we had only tropical clothing – and not much of that – all the POWs felt the cold and we started lighting small fires, especially early in the morning, to keep ourselves warm. These were lit in the open because it was danger-ous to have fires in the bamboo huts, and people huddled round the fire trying to get warm. There was still some time to go before we returned to Singapore because the Japanese had decided that we were suffering from too many infectious diseases to be allowed back into Malaya.

# CHAPTER XII

# Mac the knife

The collection of POWs in the Kanburi camp were suffering from a variety of tropical diseases. The most prevalent were malaria and tropical ulcers, and for the treatment of these the camp had a supply of drugs provided by the Japanese, probably under instructions from Singapore. There were three British medical officers from the various original groups of F and H Forces to attend the sick; other medical officers were in the camp but were themselves suffering from the common complaints.

Malaria was evident in its two common forms, namely benign tertiary (BT) and malignant tertiary (MT) forms. In each of these types there is a cycle of one day with rigors, then high fever accompanied by profuse sweating, followed by one day free of sweating but with a subnormal temperature.

Benign tertiary malaria is the form that can recur after an attack has been cured, but is a milder form of the disease. Malignant tertiary malaria does not recur, but is a severe form of the disease with a strong possibility of being fatal. In addition to the BT and MT forms of malaria there was a third type, cerebral malaria which was commonly fatal, but it had a lower incidence in the camp. Even if the patient recovered from an attack of cerebral malaria it left his brain damaged and the patient generally became mentally deranged, in some cases, severely so.

The standard treatment for malaria was quinine administered in tablet form, on a fifteen-day course. The malaria in this part of Thailand was so virulent that patients were contracting a second infection on the tenth day of the fifteen-day course.

Malaria was diagnosed by preparing a blood slide from the person suspected of being infected and, since the disease was occurring so often, every person in the camp had a permanent blood slide number. By keeping a check on these numbers, it was found that only about sixteen people in the camp did not contract the disease and, fortunately, I was one of them.

Why we sixteen people remained free from malaria was unknown, because none of us was able to take any precautions against infection. Nobody in the camp had a mosquito net, and nobody had sufficient clothing to cover up all skin surfaces at night. Mosquitoes become active at dusk, and in Thailand the species of mosquito bite until about midnight. During the day and the later part of the night the anopheline species were not active.

Only mosquitoes infected with the malarial parasite spread the disease, but with such a high concentration of infected people in the locality of the camp, the proportion of infected mosquitoes must have been high. They could bite everybody at night and so spread the disease throughout the camp.

Both amoebic and bacillary dysentery occurred in the Kanburi camp, with amoebic dysentery becoming chronic in many cases. Recovery from bacillary dysentery confers a brief immunity lasting about four months and, as there were drugs to combat the disease, there were generally fewer cases in the camp at any one time. There were so many houseflies, because of the unhygienic latrine facilities, that the spread of dysentery was almost inevitable.

There were skin complaints for which there was little treatment and, of course, tropical ulcers. The latter had to be treated by surgery and the camp had facilities for this purpose. These facilities were not ideal and would have horrified any medical man from the Western world, but at least they provided some form of treatment which was successful in a good many cases.

The camp was occupied about this time by approximately three thousand eight hundred POWs, these being the remnants of the Singapura group of ten thousand men. The Singapore commander had ordered all personnel of the group back to Singapore, but many of the men were too ill to be moved, so a further period of living in the camp had been ordered for the sick to recover. During this time more people died from malaria, dysentery and ulcers.

Not long after I had arrived at Kanburi, I met the Indian Army medical officer who was my friend at Tonchan South. He had arrived back at the base camp before me and was now busy with medical duties.

His duties were that of anaesthetist to the camp surgeon and in his spare time we used to meet and chat about the various camps we had been in. Then one day he came to see me in the afternoon and asked for my help; his anaesthetic machine had broken down. As far as he knew I was the only chemist in the camp, and he thought I might be able to repair the machine.

I went to look at the anaesthetic machine and he explained how it worked and where it was broken. I said I thought there was a possibility of repairing it, but I would need some glass tubing and some form of flame for glass blowing. He managed to get some glass tubing and a file for cutting the tubing, but all he could manage as a flame was a candle. So with the candle and the file I set to work to repair the machine. Glass blowing with a candle was not an easy task, but with patience I managed to get the tubing into the necessary shapes and lengths to fit into the machine. It did not look at all like the original and I think Heath Robinson would have been proud of my final result.

In the meantime, all operations had ceased until the patients could be anaesthetized. On the morning after I had finished my labours the previous evening I went with the medical officer to the operating theatre. As the machine was now almost unrecognizable, I had to demonstrate to him how it was operated. After a morning's work of instruction the anaesthetic part of the operations went smoothly, and I returned to my hut.

The next morning as I was finishing my breakfast of tapioca – I was still officially sick with amoebic dysentery – the camp surgeon came to the hut and explained that my Indian Army medical friend had contracted malaria and was not able to function as his anaesthetist. He asked if I was willing to become his anaesthetist. I told him that I had no idea on how to proceed with the work – particularly how to test whether a patient was unconscious or not.

He said it was easy enough to test for unconsciousness and, as I knew how to operate the anaesthetic machine and there were no other doctors available, I was the last hope. Reluctantly I agreed, wondering what the patients would think when they saw me trying to anaesthetize them.

I followed the surgeon into the operating theatre, if such a grandiose description could be applied to what I was seeing. It was a room, about twenty feet wide and about thirty feet long, at the end of a bamboo hut and had been separated from the rest of the hut by a wall. The walls had been cut in half so that they were about four feet high. The roof was made of *atap*, as usual, with no ceiling, so that it was open to the roof.

Between the low wall and the roof was stretched mosquito netting, fastened securely by strips of wood nailed to the wall and the roof. The netting was torn in places and had been repaired by sewing the ends of the tear together, using cotton thread. The door was a frame of bamboo, with the whole area covered with mosquito netting. This allowed people entering or leaving the theatre to see what was happening on the other side of the door.

The operating table was an ordinary trestle table placed in the middle of the room, with a free passage round all sides. Another table stood close by the operating table and on this the surgical instruments were placed. A third table was placed against the wall on one side of the room, and on this was assembled the variety of material, mainly cotton cloth, used for dressings in place of bandages.

The patients for operations waited on a bench outside the operating theatre, and were summoned when their turn came round. An orderly called the men, took down their names and made a record of all the operations for the day. He had a small table and chair inside the operating theatre on which to carry out his duties.

The surgical instruments were sterilized in a mobile sterilizer, a small device which was used when doctors in India went on tour. It sterilized a few instruments at a time by immersing them in boiling water, the water being heated by an alcohol burner. All the instruments, as far as possible, were sterilized in this fashion.

These details of the operating theatre I took in as we waited for the first patient to appear. When he arrived he climbed on to the operating table and I started to anaesthetize him. As soon as I thought he was unconscious the surgeon showed me how to raise an eyelid and look at his eye, to test whether he had lost consciousness. Satisfied that the patient was unconscious, he began to operate. This first operation involved scraping a tropical ulcer, and to understand what was happening a description of tropical ulcers is necessary.

A tropical ulcer has a raised lip surrounding it, the thickness being about the same as the thickness of a human lip; in fact the boundary of the ulcer is quite raised from the level of the surrounding flesh.

This raised lip is the growing point of the ulcer, and it surrounds an area of flesh covered in pus. The operation first necessitated the removal of this surrounding lip, and then the internal area had to be scraped clean of pus and damaged tissue, leaving raw flesh.

I admired the dexterity of the surgeon as he took a scalpel and with one rapid circular motion cut off the lip; this was then removed with tweezers. The pus was scraped off with a spoon until the flesh appeared clean. A dressing of sulphanilamide powder was applied to the scraped ulcer and the whole bound up with a dressing from the collection of cotton material.

The surgeon was an Australian who, I gathered, was well known in Australia for his ability in his profession. He had come to Thailand with a contingent in F Force and had now been in Kanburi for some time, carrying out many different types of operation on the POWs in the camp. Dressings were one of the major problems, as there was no supply of suitable bandages. When a patient dispensed with his dressing, usually by this time in a thoroughly dirty and contaminated state, it was put in a petrol tin with water and boiled to clean and sterilize the material. The continual boiling did not help the usefulness of the material; it slowly became thin and worn in texture and the surgeon and his aides were always looking for fresh material to use as dressings.

The team to assist the surgeon was small. A sergeant from the Volunteer force in Malaya, who had been a male theatre nurse in Singapore, was in charge of the surgical instruments and responsible for their sterilization. During an operation he handed the requisite instrument to the surgeon.

The discarded surgical refuse was put in a bucket and an orderly was responsible for burning it at the end of the operating session, in a makeshift incinerator just outside the operating theatre. In amputations, this would include the disposal of amputated limbs. Lastly, there were two people armed with fly swats to dispose of the houseflies that managed somehow to find their way into the operating theatre. However hard everybody tried, there were always some flies in the theatre, and it was essential to keep them away from the operation and the surgical instruments.

The camp was supplied with ether and chloroform for use as anaesthetics, and a mixture of four to one of ether to chloroform was used to anaesthetize patients. The supply had to be carefully husbanded because the Japanese were not overgenerous with the supply.

After practice I managed to use just 4cc of ether and 1cc of chloroform to render a patient unconscious for the scraping of an ulcer. This meant the surgeon had to operate at high speed because the patient was unconscious for only four to five minutes. In that time the ulcer lip had to be excised, the inner area scraped, the sulphanilamide powder applied to the cleaned wound and the first dressing tied over the wound. The patient generally woke up as the last dressing was being applied. One Australian, who occupied a space on the *chang* just a few feet from me, said that my efforts at anaesthetizing patients were rather like the 'twilight sleep' given to maternity patients in Australia.

The ulcers on which the surgeon operated were small, ranging from half an inch up to just over two inches across. Any ulcer which was larger was dressed, but generally necessitated amputation at some time in the future. The surgeon tried to avoid amputation if it was at all possible; he always obtained the patient's consent before operating.

A complete cure of an ulcer was effected only by excising the growing region of the surrounding lip. As long as the lip remained intact, an ulcer would continue to grow.

In many cases the patient deferred amputation as long as possible, hoping against hope that a cure would be effected. This, however, was unlikely and the deferring of the amputation meant that the operation became more serious.

The worst case of an ulcer that appeared while I was working in the operating theatre was on an Australian soldier. He had consistently refused to have his leg amputated and the ulcer had grown until it stretched from his ankle to half way up his thigh. To prevent movement of the leg, a triangular splint had been made and his leg rested in a bent position on this splint, with the knee at the top of the triangle. The ulcer had eaten away his flesh to such an extent that it was possible to insert a hand between his shin bone and the remaining calf muscle of the leg. He finally consented to have the limb amputated, but by this time the end of the ulcer was so near to his hip that the operation was difficult.

The surgeon carried out the amputation and the Australian was put back in his hut. But the constant pain of the ulcer had lowered his resistance to such an extent that he lived for only two days.

Most serious cases of tropical ulcers occurred on the legs of victims. The lack of proper clothing meant that both legs and arms were exposed, but legs were more likely to come in contact with bamboo, and occasionally other plants, when working in the jungle.

During my spell of duty in the operating theatre I took part in about twelve leg amputations and three arm amputations. After the operation the surgeon would visit the patient on his *chang* in one of the huts and comfort him as shock set in when he awoke. Occasionally I accompanied him on his rounds, which would also include the more severe cases of scraped ulcers.

The treatment of ulcers was always carried out in the morning, beginning after breakfast and finishing before lunch; the average number of cases varied between fifteen and twenty. There were just under four thousand men in camp and nearly one-third of these had tropical ulcers that needed attention, hence there was a steady stream of patients.

The men reported to the camp doctors, who sent them to the surgeon's parade which was held in the afternoon. He would decide who would be treated on the following day and this was recorded by the orderly in charge of noting admissions. After this parade the surgeon would go on his round of the huts.

The surgeon thus had a very full day, and the work went on seven days a week. I often wondered how he managed to keep going day in and day out without a respite. The other staff also had the same burden of duty, but it was not as demanding as the exacting work of operating.

Tropical ulcers did heal in some cases and when we eventually arrived back in Singapore those not responding in Thailand did heal under the better conditions. A healed ulcer, however, could still cause problems because the skin formed over the wound was only as thick as a membrane; the flesh underneath was discoloured. The membrane would break at the slightest impact, so the healed ulcer had to be protected at all times.

This was done in some cases by using a shield over the healed ulcer. Later, after release from Singapore, I met people who wore a protecting shield for several years. Any rupture of the skin led to the ulcer reforming or to the lesser complaint of a septic wound.

Amputations and other serious operations were carried out in the afternoon; this gave the patient a chance to recover while the temperature was lower at night. A bare fifty per cent survived, many dying in the first three days after the operation. The low state of health from an inadequate diet, together with the weakness caused by immobilization in a hut, were the main cause of deaths after shock. Patients with the amputation of an arm were more likely to recover than those with an amputation of a leg.

For some patients undergoing ulcer treatment the surgeon used evipan as an anaesthetic and not the ether and chloroform mixture, if it was considered unsuitable. It was used only for patients with ulcers. The patient was injected with the anaesthetic and told to count. All began 'One, two, three … ten, elev …' and were then unconscious. Only sufficient anaesthetic was given to keep him unconscious for about three to four minutes, so the surgical work had to be even quicker than with the normal routine using ether and chloroform.

One patient duly became unconscious and was in the process of having his wound dressed when we suddenly heard '… twenty-four, one hundred and twenty-five, one hundred and twenty-six – when do you want me to stop counting?' He was surprised that the operation was over, and we were surprised to hear him still counting.

There were one or two cases of abscesses, with the most serious one being on the hip. The abscess had no outlet to the skin, and when the first incision was made, the surgeon was surprised at the depth of the abscess. It was deep enough for him to put his whole hand in up to his wrist – which he had to do to remove the dead tissue and fluid in the abscess. The cavity was cleaned up and dusted with sulphanilamide and then bandaged. The patient did not recover from the operation and died. This was, probably, the most alarming operation that I witnessed. There were no surgical gloves available in the camp, so the surgeon had to plunge his naked hand into the abscess cavity, and extract the debris.

An unusual operation for the camp occurred with the incidence of two cases of appendicitis. One of the patients was the medical orderly assisting the surgeon. This left a gap in the team and we had to find another volunteer to help out until the orderly recovered enough to come back to duty. This operation was not easy to bandage, because we had no sticking plaster to keep the bandage in place. Fortunately, both appendicitis patients made a quick and full recovery.

I spent in all about five weeks acting as the unofficial anaesthetist in the theatre. After that my Indian Army doctor friend recovered from his attack of malaria and was back to work. I retired from the surgical work and thankfully went back to an ordinary POW existence.

The descriptions of the surgery may sound as if compassion was lacking. Familiarity with the everyday happenings, however, tended to dull feelings of sympathy for the patients. Most operations in which I assisted were routine and passed without recall or comment, but exceptional cases remained vividly fixed in one's memory, and these instances have been described. Serious cases evoked the thought that, but for good luck, there go I, and an immediate feeling of thank goodness I have avoided that fate so far.

There was the constant worry that such afflictions could happen to you. The result was a curious state of mind, with mixed feelings of sympathy towards the patient, worry concerning yourself, and thankfulness for good luck. Such an attitude towards living was probably common to all people in earlier times, possibly up to three hundred years ago. They lived under the circumstances of not knowing when they might fall ill, and aware there was little likelihood of a cure for serious afflictions.

The weather had become much colder just after I had finished in the theatre, and everybody felt hungrier. I decided that I should like to make cakes to supplement our diet. I had recovered from the amoebic dysentery, was pronounced fit and was back on normal rations. The food was tolerable but lacked sweetness and we all fancied something sweet after our meals.

I managed to borrow some mess tins that were not in use and built myself a small oven. The rains had stopped, so the ground was dry and building the oven in the earth caused no difficulty. Wood was easy to get, as supplies were obtained for all the cookhouse fires. I bought flour, eggs, sugar, coconut oil and ginger and started to bake ginger cakes. These I sold to the POWs who were too incapacitated to move from their places on the *chang*. The price was sufficient to cover the cost and a little over to allow for the odd cake that was not a success. Everyone who had a cake, or part of a cake, enjoyed the addition to the camp diet.

As time went on the health of the POWs in the camp improved enough for the Japanese doctors to decide we could be moved. The next stage of our period of captivity was about to begin.

# CHAPTER XIII

# Teahouse of the Third Moon

The Japanese having decided that the POWs in Kanburi were fit enough to be taken to Singapore, the first details of troops were organized. We were treated as being sick and there was no organization into companies, only contingents of six hundred men, for proceeding to Malaya. I was put in the third contingent to go by train and one morning I paraded with the assembled group, all of us having been selected as fit to travel without medical attention.

We marched to the station at Kanburi, and were loaded on to rice trucks, the same conveyance as had brought us from Malaya to Thailand. The train proceeded to Ban Pong, where we were joined to a locomotive from the Thai railway system. Ban Pong was the junction for the Burma–Thailand railway and the Thai State railway. Off we set down the line, bound apparently for Singapore, although we were unsure of our destination.

We were not so crowded on this trip, compared to the journey up from Malaya; there were only twenty or so POWs in a rice truck. We still had the bamboo stick fastened across the open doorway and the guards at each end of the train, ensuring that nobody got off. It was hardly likely that anyone would want to leave the train, as we now had enough experience to know that it would be very nearly impossible to live in the local villages.

The train started and stopped at irregular intervals, sometimes with nothing in sight, and occasionally at a rural station or even a rural halt. When we stopped, even at a halt, Thai traders appeared like magic from the surrounding countryside, scenting a trading opportunity.

They were not wrong; everyone had some Thai currency and bargains were struck for food. Unfortunately, many of the troops bought the delicious, small, very sweet, yellow bananas. Over indulgence in this fruit caused violent diarrhoea and the result was a line of bottoms hanging out over the bamboo stick at the doorway of each rice truck. The bottoms were withdrawn smartly if a train came in the opposite direction.

Meals were provided at the major stations, where there were small Thai towns. In this fashion we slowly made our way down the Kra Isthmus to the border between Thailand and Malaya. When we arrived at Padang, the border town, we exchanged the Thai locomotive for a Malayan locomotive, and set off at a smarter pace than we had experienced in Thailand. We were now obviously back under Singapore control. Eventually we arrived at Singapore station, having travelled quite quickly down Malaya, and disembarked from the train at night. There were lorries waiting for us and we were driven off to our destination.

Our contingent had arrived at a camp in Sime Road in Singapore. We descended, went into the camp and were allotted places in huts. This was indeed luxury. The huts were properly made from wood and had corrugated iron roofs. They were well maintained, had no leaks when it rained and, most surprisingly, every officer had a proper iron bed with springs and blankets. The men had similar accommodation.

Sime Road camp had been a POW camp during the initial stages of the period of our captivity when Singapore was being cleared up after the Japanese attack. Troops had been seconded from Changi and had lived in the camp. What it was originally I do not know, but it had been built as a proper camp with good accommodation, and this we inherited.

The Japanese had built three such camps after the surrender. Two of these, Sime Road camp and Havelock Road camp were for work parties engaged in the clearing of Singapore, and making it a suitable civilian area again. The third camp was at Kranji; its purpose was to build a war memorial to the Japanese who had fallen in the fight for the Malay Peninsular.

The memorial was built on a hill, created by moving a considerable amount of earth – all done by the manual labour of POWs. It followed the Eastern tradition of having cemeteries and tombs on a hill, preferably over looking some water. In Kranji, however, there was no water, only half developed jungle.

The site has now been changed to a war memorial to the Allied troops who fell in the fight against the Japanese – a development which took some time after the end of the war. The names of all those who perished in Malaya during the fighting are inscribed on the walls of a stone monument.

Around 3,800 POWs finally arrived in Sime Road camp – the remnants of the 10,000 POWs who had left Malaya in F and H Forces. The Japanese general of Singapore command, who was in charge of POWs, was determined to keep them alive in order to maintain his rank. Japanese headquarters would have liked to send us straight to Changi to join the other POWs who were still living there. But the Japanese doctors must have forbidden the transfer because we were too infectious from all our tropical complaints. In particular, the Japanese did not want the virulent form of malaria that we had brought down from Thailand, to be spread in Singapore.

The camp was strictly segregated from the residents of Singapore, being surrounded by barbed wire and closely guarded. We did not even see the persons bringing in the rations nor the traders from whom we could buy additions to our rations; any trading was done through intermediaries. We were virtually in isolation from the local inhabitants.

The POWs in the camp mustered only 3,800 because some of the original prisoners brought down from the upriver camps had died in Kanburi. There was a medical staff in Sime Road camp, consisting of the same British and Dutch medical officers who had been with the Kanburi camp. However, the staff did not include the Australian surgeon who had done so much good work there. He must have been transferred to another base camp. Subsequently I heard a rumour that he had died from septicaemia – which was possible seeing the risks he had to take by having to operate without surgical gloves. The rumour was not confirmed and, after a gap of almost forty years, I had information that the surgeon had been evacuated from Thailand to a camp at Kranji on Singapore Island.

This camp had been organized to receive the worst hospital cases from Thailand as well as some patients from Changi, and had been staffed with doctors from Changi as well as doctors from Thailand. The camp was maintained right up to the liberation of Singapore, and repatriation of patients of the Kranji hospital was organized on different lines from the repatriation of POWs from Changi.

The camp at Sime Road was divided into areas, cut off from each other by barbed wire walls. The officers' section, consisting of several huts built on the side of a hill, overlooked a gulley. On the opposite side of the gulley was a section in which were billeted Australian troops who had been part of the Singapura force.

The officers' and Australian sections were at the back of the camp and behind these two sections was scrub jungle without human habitation or cultivation. This scrub continued round the back of the officers' quarters and ran down the side of the camp.

The hill not only sloped down to the gulley but also sloped down to the section which contained the British and Dutch troops and the hospital huts. This latter section was the nearest to the road.

The British, Australian and Dutch troops were in huts built in exactly the same way as the officers' huts. Being on a hill the officers' quarters were cooler than the other quarters because of the breeze that blew over the hill.

There were separate roll calls for the sections, with just one officer in charge of each nationality of troops. From our quarters we could see the Australian roll call which was under the command of an Australian lieutenant-colonel. Japanese guards entered the camp to take charge of the roll call, but apart from that we rarely saw any Japanese, except those patrolling around the perimeter wire.

Many of the officers in the camp had come from the Indian Army and had formed part of officers' working parties in Thailand, so they had no troops to command. Those of us from the British, Australian, and Dutch armies had troops but did not exercise any command, except for the one officer in charge of roll call. There was no organization into army formations as there had been in Changi and in Thailand.

It was possible to go from one area of the camp into another, so I set off to see how many of my gunners had survived the trip to Thailand and back. I waited until the whole contingent had arrived and then visited the troop's area. I found only seventeen survivors – all that was left from the fifty-one gunners who had left Changi. This was about the average survival rate for the whole of the Singapura force.

All of these gunners survived the time in Sime Road and went on to the next stage in our travels. I was surprised that there were so few survivors. Because the men in the regiment were mainly regular soldiers I would have expected a greater number. Apparently quite a lot had died at Hin Tok when they had to work at blasting the cutting through the hills.

While in Tonchan camp I had kept a record of the gunners from my regiment who had died, noting where they were buried. These notes were written on the back of cigarette packets. The Red Bull cigarettes sold in Thailand, and purchased from the trading barges, were contained in paper packets similar to that used for American cigarettes. When the packets were opened up, they provided small sheets of notepaper and it was on such sheets that I recorded the names of those who died.

At Sime Road camp I asked the men who had returned for information about those who had died in Thailand and gradually built up a list as complete as I could. These notes were kept hidden; the Japanese were apt to deal severely with anyone discovered with handwritten material. Lists of dead soldiers would undoubtedly have caused considerable anger, as some Japanese realized that such information could be held against them should Japan lose the war. When I returned to England after liberation I copied the list and sent it to the War Office. The list was acknowledged with thanks.

One surprising thing was the enmity between the British and the Australian troops. To begin with, the bad feeling was probably engendered by the higher pay received by the Australians compared with the pay of the British troops. This feeling was similar to that aroused by the American troops in England I discovered later. We had few American POWs in Sime Road camp because the numbers who went to Thailand had not been great to start with.

A second cause of dislike arose from the fact that most of the Australian troops had not been committed to the battle on the way down the Malay Peninsular. The first time they had entered the fighting was supposed to be at a defensive position from Simpang Empat to Kluang. A road ran from Batu Pahat on the west coast of Malaya, through Simpang Empat, Kluang and on to Mersing on the east coast of Malaya. The Indian Army held Batu Pahat and Mersing and the Australians were supposed to hold the line in between these two commands.

The defensive position was organized to stop the Japanese invasion coming down the Malay Peninsular any further. It was a good position because communication along the road from Batu Pahat to Mersing allowed units to be deployed against Japanese attacks. It was the last chance of preparing a defensive position before reaching Johore Bahru at the end of the peninsular.

My regiment was at a position west of Kluang and we were supposed to support the Australians holding the line from Kluang to Simpang Empat, but we did not make contact with them. The next battle position of the Australians was on the west coast of Singapore Island, between the causeway and the south-west corner of the island. This is the point where the Japanese attacked and broke through the defences. The British troops blamed the Australians for these mishaps.

In Changi, at the start of our captivity, the British troops from India used to taunt the Indian army troops who had joined the Indian National Army by calling out '*cha wallah*' as they drove by our camp area. A *cha wallah* is the menial who dispenses tea to the troops in cantonments, so this was a deadly insult, casting aspersions on their caste as well as on their fighting prowess.

Much in the same spirit of irritating conduct the British troops reminded the Australian contingent of the social history of Australia by calling out over the wire fence 'Lift your feet well up and keep your chains off the ground'. This caused a mighty offence and it was just as well that the troops were not allowed to go from one area to another. I often wondered why the Japanese had segregated the Australians from the other troops, but no reason was given.

As the officers had no duties and no working parties to command, there was little to do other than talk, play cards, just walk round the officers' area or visit the troops' area. Entertainment was eventually organized and a small theatre constructed in the troops' area where there was more space.

The form of entertainment was mainly variety shows, with singing and other acts. We could not put on plays because there were no books available from which to produce a play. The Dutch contingent, however, supplied some very interesting turns. There were many Dutch, as opposed to Hollanders, in the camp and they provided Malay and Indonesian acts with dancing and singing such as we had not experienced before.

Before and during the Second World War there was no such country as Indonesia; it was known as the Dutch East Indies and the language spoken by the Indonesians was Malay. In Indonesia this differed little from that spoken in the Malay Peninsular, the main difference being in the use of some common words, and the use of Dutch, and not English, for loan words. Indonesian is a *lingua franca*; practically all the inhabitants speak their own indigenous language, such as Javanese or Balinese.

The outstanding contribution in the theatre was from a Javanese magician, and his shows were worthy of any audience in Europe. The first excellent show I saw involved hypnotism, and I remembered the Dutch doctor in Tonchan South. The Javanese giving the show requested a tall thin man from the audience, and an Australian volunteer came forward. He was one of the type called 'cornstalk', being very, very thin and over six feet tall.

The magician arranged three ordinary chairs in line and asked the Australian to lie on the chairs with his feet on one chair, his bottom on the second and his head on the third. He then proceeded to hypnotize him by passing his hand to and fro along his body. After a couple of minutes the Australian was hypnotized. He then withdrew the middle chair, and gradually pulled apart the two chairs at each end. In the final position the Australian was supported on the two chairs only by his heels and the back of his skull.

In this position he remained immobile, and the magician tested him to see whether he was rigid or not. He then called for the three heaviest men in the audience. Three came forward – three cooks as one would expect – and they were still definitely heavy in spite of having been working on the railway.

The magician then made the three men sit on the Australian, still extended between the two chairs – the Australian supported all three. Their combined weights could not have been less than four hundred pounds, and the Australian remained perfectly rigid the whole time. The three men returned to the audience and the magician replaced the chairs in their original position. He then woke up the Australian who had no memory of what had happened. This feat of hypnotism I could believe because it seemed feasible that a man could remain rigid under the circumstances.

The next feat I had my doubts about, although I did witness it. The Javanese took an ordinary easel, the usual triangular frame with pegs fitting in holes to support a blackboard. The magician called for a volunteer, and a soldier came forward. He was made to stand on two pegs placed on the easel about three feet above the ground and to lie back against the easel. The magician then proceeded to hypnotize him. When he was hypnotized, the magician walked round the easel to show that there was nothing behind it. He then came to the front and removed the two pegs. The soldier remained there leaning back against the easel. The pegs were replaced and the soldier woken up. He descended from the easel and he too knew nothing of what had happened. This I found too amazing to be true, yet I did see the two pegs brought forward for display. A hoax or not, it was certainly first class entertainment.

Another form of relaxation was provided by the Dutch officers who ran a canteen for the officers' area. A hut had been set aside for the canteen and it was organized as a continental cafe with tables and chairs. It sold delightful Malay, or rather Indonesian, cakes which made a welcome addition to our diet.

One cake I remember particularly was called *ongelongel* and was made from *agar* gelatin and coconut milk with a centre of *gula melaka*, the brown palm sugar. The round ball of gelatin, about an inch across, was dusted with coconut scrapings. These cakes were delicious and were a firm favourite of all who went to the canteen. There were other kinds of cakes, which were very tasty but not as good.

The officers were paid with the usual Japanese deductions, although we received no paper. I received thirty yen a month, as in Thailand. All officers paid ten yen into a mess fund, which provided welcome extras to the rations.

The pay gave spending power for the canteen which also sold cigars and cigarettes; any profit from the canteen went to the mess fund. This fund bought extra food, in particular providing fruit and coffee, which the Dutch preferred to the green tea supplied with the rations.

We stayed in Sime Road camp for about two to three months while we recovered from our infectious diseases. The Japanese had decided that the main camp at Changi was going to be reduced in size, and the POWs accommodated either in or near to Changi Gaol; since the surrender, the civilian internees had been accommodated in the gaol. Now they were going to be sent to Sime Road camp after we had left for Changi.

The internees included women and children, although the male civilians greatly outnumbered them. When the army had retreated over the causeway joining Singapore to the mainland, the government had decided to evacuate women and children. An announcement was made at the beginning of February to the effect that all women and children who wished to be evacuated should report to the Town Hall in Singapore. But some of the women decided to stay with their husbands and to keep their children with them. They believed that Singapore was impregnable – and in any case the island would be relieved as soon as possible. Those who thought otherwise attended the meeting at the Town Hall.

The evacuation was in the charge of a naval commander, who addressed the assembled civilians. His first question was 'Are there any women with seven or more children to be evacuated?' One woman put up her hand and her name and number of children was written down. The next question was 'Are there any women with six children?' A few women put up their hands, and their names were written down. Next 'Are there any women with five children?' Before the commander could get an answer a young, female, American voice piped up from the back of the hall, 'Say what chance is there on this boat for a virgin?' I never heard the answer.

The boat with the women and children selected sailed from Singapore and managed to get to India safely. After the initial evacuation other evacuations by boat were organized right up to about five days before the fall of Singapore. But these voyages were not so successful; the Japanese Air Force patrolled the seas surrounding Singapore and bombed them.

Men living in Singapore and joining the Volunteer forces had wives on these boats and never learnt their wives' fate until they returned to the UK.

Some of the women escaped from the bombed boats and tried to make their way from Sumatra to India, but the Japanese invaded Sumatra and the women were captured and interned.

The Japanese in charge of the Sime Road camp informed us that women and children were to be accommodated in the officers' section of the camp, and civilian men would be in the sections occupied by the troops. It was decided that the officers should provide some funds to decorate the canteen for the women and children.

These funds were duly collected and two artists were asked to create suitable decorations for the canteen; one of the artists was Ronald Searle and the other was a Hollander. They chose as a theme 'Eating through the Ages' and set to work. Their first drawing was of cavemen gnawing bones and suitably clad in skins. Another that was superbly depicted was of Henry VIII at a Tudor feast, brilliantly drawn and colourful. The last drawing was of the year 2000AD, with food in the form of pills and the inhabitants of the dining room owing more to science fiction than to realistic artistry.

These drawings were placed round the main room of the canteen and made a wonderful background. Other rooms had straightforward children's illustrations, making the whole area very bright. We presumed the children enjoyed the decorations but as we never came into contact with any of the women and children, we never found out their reaction.

The last addition to the decorations was made just before everyone was transported to Changi. A count was made and it was found that just over 3,200 were left of the original 10,000 troops and officers sent to Thailand in F and H Forces. This number was incorporated in the artwork so that it was not obvious.

A note for the internees benefit said that when the civilians were eventually repatriated they should convey the information back to the UK. This was done because nobody was sure that the POWs would survive any effort to retake Singapore. During our stay in Sime Road there was a dearth of news because there was no radio in the camp. We had no idea about how the war was proceeding or how long we would remain in captivity. As the remnants of F and H Forces were not that healthy, the information was left on the walls of the canteen to make sure the West would learn of the treatment of POWs in Thailand.

We were now ready to return to the original camp in Changi.

# CHAPTER XIV

# Strangers in paradise

The Japanese transported the POWs of Sime Road camp back to Changi by lorry. The move was made by day and the whole transportation took a couple of days to empty the camp. A small working party was left behind to clear up ready for civilian internees to occupy it.

Driving through Singapore town we noticed that all the cars and lorries had huge cylinders on the backs of the vehicles. This was to provide a supply of producer gas by blowing air over hot charcoal. The gas replaced petrol for civilian vehicles, petrol obviously being in short supply; only Japanese transport vehicles were using petrol. Apart from the strange appearance of the vehicles the town looked quite normal, with the usual crowd of inhabitants, busy with their day's work.

After we left the town the road to Changi passed through villages and these appeared more neglected than we had remembered them from our first arrival in Singapore. This was the road up which we walked from the town to Changi on our first day of captivity. As the vehicles drove through little interest seemed to be shown by the inhabitants at the sight of European POWs in lorries, which was rather surprising. The lorries finally arrived at the entrance to Changi camp, right by the gaol, and drove through the barbed wire entrance. Once inside we recognized our former quarters, especially those who had been in 11th Indian Division, as this was the nearest area to the entrance. The huts were deserted and there was no sign of any POWs in the area.

The same observation was made as we entered the next areas where the Australians and 18th Division had been quartered. The lorries passed the hospital area, which was still the same, situated in old army barracks. The convoy then entered the old Southern Area, where I had been billeted in Changi village, before leaving Malaya to go to Thailand.

We arrived at deserted bungalows, formerly the married quarters of the Royal Navy. A bungalow out East is not the single-storey house as understood in England, but a detached house of usually two storeys. The word is derived from Urdu or Hindustani and is used for an average size house; in these languages it is *bungala*. In India it describes living accommodation somewhere between a cottage and a mansion.

Each lorry load was allotted to a bungalow and we went in to a bare house which was to provide only accommodation. There was a mess bungalow, where our entire contingent had to go for food. Our clothing and other belongings were still very meagre, and there were no beds or bunks for us in the bungalow. We had to sleep on concrete floors, not a comfortable situation considering our lack of clothing.

The grounds around the bungalow were extensive because the married quarters of the Navy afforded very luxurious accommodation, compared to that provided for armed forces in England. The grounds had been well maintained for two reasons, firstly to provide light work for the troops in the camp so that they could earn some pay. Secondly, and most important, to avoid rain water collecting in any thick undergrowth, so that mosquitoes were denied breeding places. Sanitation control of anopheline mosquitoes, by eliminating their breeding sites, was important to reduce the incidence of malaria and the Japanese had continued this important health work.

When everyone had settled in their new accommodation, they took stock of the situation. We were once again in civilized surroundings. Sime Road camp had been a halfway house between the jungle conditions of Thailand and the relatively civilized conditions in Changi. Even so, everybody felt strange in the new surroundings; it was such a change from the rough and ready style of living in the jungle camps.

We had become used to no longer having to go out on working parties, but, as we were so dispersed over several bungalows, we all became slightly lonely. Each bungalow was in a compound, or garden, about an acre or more in extent, so from very crowded conditions we had entered very spacious conditions, and we had difficulty in making the necessary adjustment. Our quarters were not as comfortable as those in Sime Road camp, but we had more space in which to live.

Slowly we came into contact with the POWs who had been in Singapore for the whole of their stay. They had all benefited by remaining in Changi, because when a contingent of POWs went off from Changi to another destination they had shed their surplus belongings. The senior residents of the camp were thus well endowed with worldly goods, and they did not view us with any favour. They realized that some of their belongings should be shared with us poorer mortals.

An appeal was launched, some clothing was spared for us and we started to look slightly less ragged and unkempt. It was surprising just how much clothing and personal belongings had been brought into Changi when the army had originally entered the camp. In Thailand we had been provided with large quantities of rice to enable the troops to carry out the hard work required for the railway. In Sime Road camp we had been supplied with a similar quantity of rice to maintain our health. In Singapore, however, rice was in short supply and we felt hungry on the reduced rations.

Malaya had never produced sufficient rice to be self-supporting, and imported rice, mainly from Thailand, but also from Burma. Both of these countries were now not supplying enough rice to Malaya, because transport was scarce for civilian purposes. Boats from Burma were under attack from the Allied Forces, and the Malayan railway system was needed for Japanese army purposes. So, both the inhabitants of Singapore and the POWs were on short rice rations. As time went on the rations were going to become even shorter.

The result of all this was a mixed collection of feelings. The food was short, the sleeping conditions were poor, but the surroundings were good and no demands were made on us for work. All in all, a confusing situation for the ex-Thailand POWs.

I had not been too long in Changi before I suffered an attack of diarrhoea. The attack gradually became worse, so I reported to the medical officer who was in charge of our contingent of POWs. He sent me to the hospital, where a specimen was demanded. I was given an old tin hat and told to provide the necessary evidence. This I did, and waited while it was analysed.

It was confirmed that I had bacillary dysentery. How I had contracted the disease was a mystery but there it was and I was duly admitted to hospital. Compared to conditions in Thailand this really was a hospital. I had a good bed, sheets and even the luxury of a mosquito net. There were orderlies available to supply bed pans, which I needed frequently, and a doctor who visited the ward regularly.

Medical drugs were still in short supply so I received the standard treatment of Epsom salts to purge away the dysentery. The salts worked and I began to recover. While I was doing this my friends, who had been with me in Sime Road camp, came to visit me, using the bus system which was still in operation.

This was the bus system of an officer with a flag marching a group of men from one area to another, in this case the bus from Southern area to the hospital area. My friends gave me the welcome news that D-day had taken place and that Allied troops had landed in France.

The news was a great boost to our morale. When we had met the POWs who had stayed in Changi we had been brought up to date on the progress of the war. The fighting in the Far East did not seem to be going a quickly as we would have welcomed, although it was realized that the great distances in the Pacific and the idea of island hopping would mean that it would take a considerable time to defeat the Japanese. The landings in Italy had promised a quickening of the pace of the war, but now progress there appeared to have slackened.

With the invasion of the Continent we had hopes that the war would speed up, and our captivity might be approaching an end. Our elation was not suppressed, because there were no Japanese troops in the POW areas to notice our reaction to the news.

After a fairly short stay in the hospital I was discharged as fit and returned to my quarters in the bungalow. I was not long there when a new complaint made itself felt; it was toothache. Any complaints with teeth had always been a nightmare when in Thailand as there was only one dentist in all of the POW camps, as far as I knew. He had been a dentist with my regiment when we first went into Changi, and he had left on an earlier party.

The dentist did not have any contact with the Singapura groups and any trouble with teeth had to be attended to by one of the doctors. Treatment was therefore primitive, especially with no local anaesthetic; that is why hypnosis had been used in Tonchan South camp.

However, there were two dentists in Changi, and off I went to see one of them. Both had been in private practice before the war in Singapore, and had become POWs because they had joined the Singapore Volunteer forces.

The dentist examined my teeth and said I needed a filling in one of them. The equipment for drilling teeth was a primitive drill, worked by a foot treadle. The speed of rotation of the drill was not high and it took a long time to drill a respectable hole. No local anaesthetic was available, so it was a somewhat lengthy and painful procedure.

The drilling was finished at last and the dentist proceeded to make up the filling and insert it in the tooth. After examining it carefully he told me it had been a troublesome job and would I go back to see him in two day's time. When I reported back he examined the tooth carefully, then asked me if it had caused any pain when I ate or drank anything hot. I had experienced no pain and told him so.

He was very relieved and I then heard that the filling had been an experiment. The dentists had exhausted the supply of dental amalgam so they had decided to make their own supply. They had acquired the Perak Golf Trophy, a large ornamental silver cup, and melted it down. After mixing it with other ingredients they then had a new supply of dental amalgam. The only difficulty was whether the coefficient of expansion of the silver was the same as that of a human tooth.

Fortunately the silver amalgam that they had made and a human tooth did have the same expansion, otherwise my tooth would have split and been exceedingly painful. It was just as well that I did not know I was the subject of an interesting experiment. I was told to have the tooth refilled on my return to England, which I did.

When all the civilian internees had left Changi Gaol, a contingent of POWs moved in to prepare the camp for the rest of the men. After cleaning the gaol, they came in working parties back to the original camp and proceeded to demolish the huts that had previously supplied accommodation for the POWs. This was done by removing the roofs in sections, then dismantling the walls. All the huts had been built in sections to a standard army engineers' plan, making it easy to split the huts back into the same sections.

These sections were transported by truck down to the gaol and erected to form huts, which were placed at the back of the gaol and down its west side. The area was then enclosed with a barbed wire fence. Huts were also erected for additional guards on the east side of the gaol, near to the original warders' houses. Lookout towers at each of the corners of the building were manned by guards.

The gaol area was now ready to receive the rest of the POWs, and we were marched down to the gaol and accommodated in the newly erected huts. The POW areas, other than Southern area and the hospital barrack block, had now been almost cleared of huts. The remainder of the Southern area camp was emptied and the hospital moved into the gaol.

There were still many men attending the hospital as out-patients, since the war casualties continued to require attention. Amputations that did not heal properly and required further surgery, wounds that refused to heal, all needed constant care.

The POWs were now entering on the last stretch of their captivity – with some hope of seeing an end to the war.

# CHAPTER XV

# The Changi Ritz

The group I was in arrived at Changi Gaol after marching down from Southern area, and was separated into officers and other ranks. The officers were allocated a hut where we found double bunks, made of wood with wire mesh, awaiting us. I chose a lower bunk and put my belongings on it. The hut filled up and we all looked round to see who our new neighbours were.

We were a very mixed collection, a mixture of the remnants of F and H Forces and the long-time residents of Changi. There were officers from the Indian Army, from the original garrison of Singapore, some from the 18th Division, some who had been captured in Java, and some from the Volunteer forces.

The next important item to investigate was the arrangements for sanitation. There were showers – about half a dozen on a concrete platform – and some stand pipes from which you could collect water if you had a receptacle. The water was turned on at six o'clock in the evening and everybody rushed to get a shower and, hopefully, wash some clothes.

The water supply, however, was erratic; it stopped and started for no apparent reason. Just when everyone had applied soap, the water would stop, and we all stood hopefully waiting for the water to come on again, while the soap dried on our bodies. This occurrence was accompanied by some very descriptive language of the Japanese Army engineers. Apart from such inconveniences, the showers were a delight after our previous experiences of lack of water in Thailand.

Two types of latrine were available, boreholes and urinals. The boreholes were made by drilling with an auger to make a hole about one foot in diameter and twenty feet deep. This hole had a wooden cover with a flap that lifted up, sealing off the hole from the outside. To use it, one had to squat, but by this time we were all used to squatting and, in fact, now preferred it. Squatting was essential if you were going to use a bottle and not paper.

The advantage of a borehole is that, with normal use, it lasts for about six months before becoming too full to use. It will digest its contents and be available for use in a few months time, depending on the kind of soil.

The urinals were also boreholes, but this time completely covered with a wooden board through which went a metal pipe leading down into the hole. At the top of the tube was an inverted lampshade sealed on to the pipe. This was an excellent hygienic urinal, and the use of boreholes and urinals prevented the spread of enteric diseases in the camp around Changi Gaol.

Our first couple of months in the gaol camp were spent in idleness, there being no work other than simple camp duties carried out by the troops to earn some pay. After this initial period the Japanese started the construction of an aerodrome near Changi point. For this, working parties were formed, composed of troops under the command of an officer. The work was hard, as the ground mainly consisted of a swamp; the vegetation had to be cleared, the land drained and then filled in. Construction of the aerodrome lasted from the end of 1944 up to the summer of 1945, but, as far as I know, the aerodrome was never used by the Japanese Air Force.

With the troops engaged on the aerodrome a variety of light work in the camp had to be carried out by other people, including the officers. In this way I became engaged in the interesting job of plaiting lavatory screens. These screens were made from the leaves of the coconut palm.

Five or six coconut palm leaves were placed side by side, so that the fronds of one leaf lay over the fronds of its neighbour. A frond of one leaf was then woven above and below the fronds of its neighbour until it reached the midrib of the neighbour, then it was folded back on itself and tucked in, following the weaving pattern. The result was a diagonal mesh of palm fronds between two midribs, the top of the palm leaf being cut off to the correct height, and the bottom being the trimmed base of the midrib.

The width of the screen was determined by the number of palm leaves, and made to fit the location of the screen round a lavatory. Whilst busily engaged in this exercise, my friend working next to me remarked: 'When your son asks you "What did you do in the war, daddy?" you'll have the perfect answer.'

'Yes' I said, 'and what will that be?'

'I plaited lavatory screens, son, and was given a medal for it.'

We both laughed and discussed the medal we all thought we would be given for the Malayan campaign, which by popular consensus was to be designed as crossed running shoes in yellow on a green background.

There were many other types of light duties, some particularly suited to the war casualties. There were small factories making toothbrushes out of coconut fibres and pieces of wood. Such things were necessary, because, after nearly three years, all our personal belongings of this nature had worn out. Ladles and drinking cups were made from coconut husks, and when polished looked quite decorative. One little factory made soap, as buying soap on the local market was too expensive. Both the local yellow Chinese soap and the soap manufactured in the camp were crude products, and were probably the cause of some of our skin complaints. Brushes for sweeping were made from dried grass and bamboo, useful in keeping the huts clean. There was even a tailoring service, mending old uniforms or cutting them up to make new garments. Much ingenuity was exhibited in attempting to produce all the goods which were now in short supply.

An industrial chemist and a dietician worked together to brew alcohol from lalang, the very coarse grass that grows in Malaya. The main difficulty was reducing the grass to a powder which could be fermented. This was achieved by putting the grass in a five-gallon drum with a collection of old nuts and bolts, and rotating the drum on an axle. The continuous motion reduced the grass to a fine powder.

There were plenty of yeast spores floating about in the air and, eventually, a strain was captured which fermented the grass powder. A weak alcoholic mixture was obtained and this was distilled in a primitive still, formed from odd pipes, tubes, and other motor car parts. The resulting alcohol was used by the medical department; I occasionally gave a hand with this particular work. Entertainment was provided in the camp by a theatre group. The library had been brought down from the Southern area camp so there were plenty of books available for the production of plays. The plays, of course, required the requisite costumes, and here another friend of mine was in charge of the wardrobe.

Many people had come into the camp with a strange assortment of clothes, musical instruments, and other impedimenta. As people had been drafted on contingents to go overseas, their belongings had been left to the people remaining behind. In this way some people had acquired a respectable collection of odds and ends.

The problem was to keep track of this wealth of material, and here my friend had his system. He designed cards on which was written the person's name and his particular possessions. Holes were cut accurately round the edge of these cards so that the holes all lined up when the cards were put in a pack. Specific holes were further cut so that when a skewer was inserted through the holes, those cards specially marked would fall out. There would be a hole for evening dress, so that cards of people possessing an evening dress would fall out from the pack. The type of evening dress would then be ascertained, from the written details on the card, including its measurements, and the person then contacted to provide clothes for a particular production. Occasionally, when work was slack, we would have fun with these wardrobe cards. We would look for a person with a bowler hat, black stockings and a trombone. Surprisingly, with such an odd collection of gear, a name would appear and we would go round to his hut to check whether we were right and ask him how he had managed to get such an odd assortment of possessions.

There were some talented musicians in the camp and, as well as presenting new arrangements of existing tunes, they also composed original tunes, all of which were presented on the stage, in musical reviews and in new plays written in the camp. The play *The Dover Road* was one of the best performances given in the theatre, with good acting, excellent costumes and scenery. There was thus no lack of entertainment provided in the camp and, with a large potential audience, a system of tickets was organized to fill the accommodation in the theatre.

The theatre itself consisted of a stage with wings and dressing rooms and the seats were formed from coconut palm trunks, some cut to one and a half feet as stands, with split trunks laid on top to provide bench seats. The whole theatre area was surrounded by palm leaf screens such as I had previously plaited. These screens enabled a show to be given with only the audience allowed to see it. The stage and connected rooms were built as a hut, with a decorated arch around the stage; it had an atap roof to protect the rooms, used for storage, and the stage. The audience sat on the bench seats in the open, shaded by some coconut palms in the auditorium.

All the productions were presented in the evening, after we had eaten the evening meal, starting about seven o'clock. This allowed the lights on the stage to be used efficiently; sunlight would have destroyed the lighting effects. As it seldom rained in the evening, this was an ideal time to present a show. If it did rain, as occasionally happened, the show was called off and the audience retired back to their huts. A system of booking ensured that everyone had a chance to see each show.

Many of the plays had female parts and some of the POWs started to specialize in these parts. Such parts needed costumes, and although many curious items had been brought into Changi by the officers and men, female costumes was not among them. All dresses for female parts, therefore, had to be made in the camp. They were created by the tailoring service, which became very proficient in sewing costumes for the productions.

Living conditions in the camp had remained the same for the troops; they received neither pay nor rations when sick. The camp provided work in the various small workshops manufacturing necessities for the POWs, and men working in these workshops received pay. This allowed many of the disabled to earn pay and receive rations.

Men engaged on working parties on the aerodrome were also paid. There were, however, a number of POWs who were still too sick or too disabled to work, and so it was necessary to provide them with food and some pay. The original system, devised by the senior officers, was continued and all officers contributed sixteen dollars a month for the benefit of the sick. Our net pay, after Japanese deductions, was now forty dollars a month. This deduction was recorded in our Pass Books; I still have mine.

This left twenty-four dollars spending money which, when we were in the camp at the start of our captivity, was sufficient to meet our daily needs. Now, however, prices had risen and the amount to spend had to be carefully budgeted. Inflation was beginning to be felt, and not only in the POW camp but also by the civilians in Singapore.

Towards the end of 1944, some Red Cross parcels made their first appearance in the camp. This was a very welcome sight, but the distribution left a lot to be desired; it worked out at about one parcel per fifteen persons. While the parcels were appreciated, they produced problems such as how to divide a half-pound slab of chocolate between fifteen men. A strict division pro rata would mean losing a part of the chocolate in the division and each man's portion would be too small either to enjoy or even to see.

The problem was solved initially by putting every item into cakes, pies, or other culinary efforts and then dividing the offering into fifteen portions. Unfortunately, the group to which I belonged had seventeen persons and, as I was a scientist, I had the task of dividing the cake or pie into seventeen portions. With a round cake this is difficult, but with a rectangular cake it is almost impossible. I attempted the task, carefully watched by sixteen pairs of calculating eyes, eager to see a slip and make capital out of it.

The parcels did not arrive that often, maybe one every two or three weeks, and then the task of division would arise. After several nerve-racking divisions of cakes and pies I suggested an alternative. I would divide the cake or pie into twenty pieces everyone would get his share and seven lucky people would get two shares.

A roster would then be established and would move down the seventeen each time we had a share out. This was accepted as a good idea, and we cut cards for the order of the roster. The next step was how to record the roster. One member had the bright idea of using a cribbage board, numbered against the roster, with four rosters for different categories, such as one for sweet cakes, one for savoury pies, one for sweets or similar countable offerings, and one for cigarettes.

The system worked magnificently and all were happy. There was an element of chance in the draw, depending on the contents of the Red Cross parcel, but this made it more exciting and something to look forward to in what was otherwise a monotonous existence.

However, one day tragedy struck. A clumsy member of the seventeen-man group dropped the cribbage board and all the pins fell out. There was consternation and furious arguments as to where the pins had been when the accident happened. The matter was finally settled, but one or two members of the group were not on speaking terms for several weeks after the incident.

This method of giving any excess food to people on a roster was used by all the cookhouses, and it was known as the 'leggy queue', the word 'leggy' being a corruption from the Malay word *lagi* which means 'more in addition' as opposed to 'more than' as in more than two hundred. Our cribbage board was known as the leggy board.

When we were in the huts around the gaol, the whole camp, gaol and huts was under the command of a Japanese lieutenant whose name was Takahashi. He lived outside the camp and employed POWs to maintain his house and compound. He had a very pretty Malay mistress, with whom he apparently was deeply in love. To show his affection he decided to build a pleasure pavilion of the type common in the East.

A fortunate site must always have 'good wind and water' so the pavilion was built on stilts out in the sea beyond low tide, with a bridge leading from the land to the pavilion. The troops working on this project were mainly Australians, and they took their time over the work in hand. It was pleasant work and they saw no need to hurry it. Eventually the pavilion was finished and Takahashi and his mistress enjoyed their new surroundings.

In the meantime the Malay girl had become pregnant and Takahashi was proud of his prowess. The infant was duly born and then there was trouble; the infant was obviously Eurasian. Takahashi was furious and demanded to know who was responsible, but everybody remained silent. Not finding the culprit, Takahashi showed his displeasure by stopping the cigarette ration of the POWs for one month. This was serious news indeed, and if we had found the culprit, who we strongly believed was an Australian, he would have been lynched.

Early on in spring 1945 I was put in charge of a hut containing one hundred men. The hut was the first one near the perimeter fence, bordering on the road on the west side of the gaol. I nominated the men for working parties to see that all had a fair chance of working and getting paid. I did not go out on any of these parties, but remained in camp to oversee the hut.

One day Lieutenant Takahashi was summoned to Tokyo and faced a problem. Since giving up his Malay mistress he had adopted a monkey. He could not take the monkey with him and he did not trust anyone in his quarters to look after the monkey, so he decided to leave it in the charge of one of the POWs. As I was nearest to the perimeter wire, he thought this gave the monkey the best chance of living, so it was put in my charge.

This was a terrific responsibility, remembering the loss of the cigarette ration for the failure of his mistress to reserve herself for Takahashi. It was a greater responsibility than most realised, because the men in the camp were very hungry and any chance of a meat meal was very tempting. I deputed three men to be in charge of the monkey and inspected the guardians every few hours. I insisted they slept with the monkey tied to their waists because otherwise the monkey would certainly be lost to a passing thief.

At that time there were several pets in the camp, especially dogs. Anybody who owned a dog also slept with it tied to his waist, so that he was aware of any attempt to steal it. A stray dog walking by a hut would be skinned and in the pot within ten minutes; the camp inhabitants were very hungry.

The monkey was thus carefully guarded as I did not wish her to end up in a stew. My arrangements worked satisfactorily and I was relieved to hand the monkey back to Takahashi on his return from Tokyo. But during the period of guarding the animal I had had a lot of time to study the antics of monkeys. The monkey was a female – there was nothing queer about Takahashi – and so clung to her male guards. I do not think a male monkey would have survived the experience. She was greedy, wily, and playful, and we became fond of her, and almost sorry to say goodbye.

When I took up the position of being in charge of the hut I was transferred to a new mess. I moved in and awaited my first meal. To my surprise the senior officer asked 'Are you one of those officers with caliper eyes?' This I could hardly deny; like all POWs I could gauge the size of any dish with great accuracy. So I could only reply 'Not more so than most of the people in camp.'

News of the Allied landings in Europe had given us a new lease of life and a desire to catch up on the years being wasted in captivity. Courses were started for anybody who wished to participate. Academic courses were available up to university standard.

I took part in chemistry courses and lectured on the subject, using the books available in the library. Paper was in short supply, which reduced any work on a subject to oral presentation. I enjoyed the mental stimulation of having to prepare a lecture or talk and the students had the satisfaction of knowing that they were preparing themselves for work after liberation.

News was now plentiful, and the organization for its dissemination was as near foolproof as was possible. I attended a group of POWs with one person giving an account of the BBC news bulletin every day. This I had to learn by heart and, by the end of the stay in Changi, most of us could hear and repeat accurately a full twenty minutes of reported news.

I then went to another group where I was the dispenser of news and the others digested the report and learnt it. This procedure was repeated and I was also a member of another group, so I could check on the accuracy with which the news was being passed down the line of communication. The organization for dispensing the news was based on the principle of the communist cells. If any one person was interrogated and gave away the name of the news spokesman, that spokesman, in turn, would give the name of his spokesman, but the Japanese would go round and round the various overlapping circles. It would be almost impossible to locate the actual head of the cell network.

Details of the naval battles in the Pacific Ocean were remembered with great accuracy and I was surprised how little variation there was by the time I attended my second news group. The news of the Japanese war obviously interested us more than the news on the European fronts, and we followed the island-hopping campaign in the Pacific with great interest – at the same time vastly improving our knowledge of geography.

It was not until I returned to England and had been home for about two months that I discovered the source of the news in the Changi Gaol camp. The original source was one of the students to whom I taught chemistry, so probably I was in the very first group to receive the news. Presumably, there must have been a few senior officers who had instigated the reception of news and the cell organization for spreading it.

The radio operator slept on a charpoy, an Indian bed with four thick legs, each about six inches square, and a framework on which a string net provided the bed. The radio was hidden in one of the legs and was operated by a switch which was a knot in the wood. Another knot was exactly in front of a loudspeaker, and to listen in to the radio the operator held a stethoscope to the knot. The radio was completely disguised and only the actual sight of the operator using the stethoscope would have revealed it.

The Japanese were aware that news was filtering through to the POWs because there was an undercurrent of wellbeing when the news was good and the converse when the news was either poor or uninteresting. Surprise searches of the huts were conducted, both by day and by night, to try to catch the radio operator, but never succeeded.

Although the news was improving as the days went on, the war was obviously still a long way from reaching Singapore or anywhere near it. The Japanese were in control of the whole of modern Indonesia, and the nearest fighting to us was in the Andaman Islands. The landing at Leyte in the Philippines gave us hope that the war was coming our way, but then Allied forces turned away and headed for Okinawa, leaving us out of the strategic advance.

The fighting in Burma was getting near Rangoon but there seemed little hope of the XIVth Army reaching Malaya for some considerable time.

# CHAPTER XVI

# Confucius – he say

From my vantage point in the hut near the perimeter wire I could see that the transport arriving at the gaol was becoming scarcer and all vehicles were now using the large cylinders generating gas from charcoal. The petrol shortage was getting severe and this had the effect of reducing the amount of food supplied to the camp.

The rice ration was reduced to five ounces per man per day, which is less than the normal requirement for an individual. The supply of vegetables was reasonable, being supplemented by produce from the gardens maintained by the POWs, and we were being issued with more fish. The two useful items of fish were shark and giant ray; shark makes an excellent meal, as does ray; both are cartilaginous fish with firm, solid flesh.

Giant rays arrived whole at the camp. The fish were diamond shape, about six feet long by about five feet wide, with a corresponding thickness of flesh. They had very long tails – I estimated up to twenty feet long – with a nasty looking barb at the end. The fish were cut up in the camp, and distributed to the cookhouses.

With the shortness of rations everybody dreamt of food; it was also in our thoughts whenever we were awake. Along with others, I used to talk to people who had spent their lives out East, about the various oriental dishes and the way of cooking them. I even remember with delight the recipe for fried duck skin. All these words of culinary information were written down on odd scraps of paper, hopefully for use when we were freed.

The experience of semi-starvation caused us to be determined that we would never go hungry again. We all decided that, on our return to England, we would indulge in four square meals a day. Food became an obsession, and we learnt to hate the thought of food being wasted. With this view went the accompanying thought that water should not be wasted, and I – and I think most other POWs – could not bear to see a tap running without the water being used. However long ago we experienced the shortage of food and water, the two hatreds of waste exist still today, personally speaking, and I think all ex-POWs would be in agreement.

The Japanese had issued a currency for Malaya, with notes for all denominations, the unit being a dollar, divided into one hundred cents. There were even notes for denominations for cents, not that such notes would buy much. The characteristic feature of the notes was a banana tree on each side of the bank-note, and the money was derisively called '*wang pisang*' in Malay which is 'banana money'. The notes were easy to forge and rumour had it that many Chinese had a printing press in a back room and were churning out the bank-notes like confetti.

We gathered later that the British government had helped in this process of increasing the supply of money, by flooding the country with bank-notes dropped from aeroplanes to the guerrilla troops in the jungle. Whoever was responsible for all the extra money, the result was inflation on a scale unimaginable. When we first entered Changi a coconut cost four cents; it now cost fifty-five dollars, so a small share of a coconut was all that could be managed from our pay each month.

Tobacco cost thirty-five dollars an ounce, and cigars and cigarettes were well beyond our spending power. Two or three POWs would club together to buy an ounce of tobacco and then share it amongst them. We adopted the Chinese method of rolling a cigarette with the paper in the form of a cone, the apex being placed in the mouth, so that as little tobacco as possible was wasted at the end of a smoke. The experience of inflation in Singapore stayed with us for a long time and even now is one of the frightening thoughts of present life.

There was a little spare ground in the camp area near the huts, and some POWs managed to keep chickens, closely guarded, as the eggs were an important supplement to the diet. One day a friend invited me to a chicken curry. I was surprised, because I thought he had given up keeping chickens. He said he hadn't, so late in the evening along I went to his hut, and joined some others for the chicken curry.

The curry was delicious and I enjoyed every mouthful. When I had finished I was chatting to one of the others who had also enjoyed the meal, and asked him where the chickens were now being kept. He replied 'We gave up keeping chickens last month, it wasn't chicken, it was rat.' I immediately felt uncomfortable and rushed out and vomited. I was furious with myself at losing all that good protein, but the thought of eating rat was just too much, however hungry I felt.

The spices for the curry had come from the black market; several of the POWs were escaping through the wire at night and buying food and other goods from the Chinese in the vicinity. This was a dangerous occupation, because if caught, the penalty could be severe.

The men engaged in the black market had started business by selling their personal belongings, such as watches, Parker pens, and rings, to the guards, who were always on the lookout for Rolex watches and goods of similar quality. Those men who had begun in the black market, had contacted agents in Singapore town through the local Chinese, who had continued to live in their villages and hamlets within the main perimeter wire of Changi camp.

Through these agents, local produce was available – at a price. Popular items were *Ikan bilis*, a kind of whitebait – a good source of protein and calcium – which cost about thirty-five dollars a pound, and *belachan,* which was dried prawn paste. *Belachan* is made by pounding small shrimps into a paste, wrapping the paste in palm leaves and burying the bundle in sand on the sea shore for several months. The resultant flavour is that of cheese mixed with rotten fish.

The *belachan* is fried and mixed with rice; our mouths would water if we smelt it frying. As a flavouring for rice, *belachan* was excellent, but after the war was over, I no longer fancied it. This shows how much hunger affects one's taste in food. Extra items of food, such as those described, were cooked on individual fires in the prison compound.

Some of the black marketeers were willing to change cheques for banana money, with the highest rate of exchange at two banana dollars to a pound sterling. Even at this rate it was occasionally worthwhile to get some money by issuing a sterling cheque, because you were never sure that you would return to the UK to enjoy the balance accumulating in your bank account.

There were a few working parties going to Singapore for the purpose of clearing up areas which needed maintenance. One of these working parties was busy near the dock area of Singapore when there was a daylight air raid. The men in the working party saw American B29 bombers attacking the harbour, with the bombs causing damage in the harbour area. On their return to Changi we had a first hand report of the air raid.

This air raid was some time in early summer 1945, and we waited impatiently for it to be reported on the news. But the raid was not mentioned and we realized that Malaya was not very high on the priority of the media – or on the Allies' plans of attack – in South East Asia. Yet it was the first indication that Malaya was a target, even if a minor one, and gave us hope that the war in the East was speeding up.

Working parties now went to clear up the bomb damage. The Chinese population was also cheered by the raid, and the local inhabitants were becoming more friendly as they could see that the Japanese were probably going to be defeated.

All POWs were warned not to mention any reference to the war when Japanese troops were about, just in case they should understand what was under discussion. Any reference to the Japanese government was disguised by reference to the Emperor, called '*Tenno Haika*' in Japanese – as far as one could guess the correct pronunciation and spelling of a name not seen in print. The initials TH were transformed into Toc H, an allusion to the Christian group formed during the First World War.

Any reference to the Japanese was given as Toc H, so any Japanese listening to a conversation and inquiring about the subject under discussion would be told it was about religion. As the Japanese respected religions of all kinds, such an answer removed any suspicion of the discussion. The news from Europe was now improving every time we listened to a bulletin. We heard that the Allies had crossed the Rhine and invaded Germany. We listened to the description of the fall of Berlin, and probably knew more about it than many people in the UK, because we were repeating the news verbatim by this time, having had so much practice.

The report of VE day was a cause for rejoicing, as we realized that the whole of the Allied effort would now be turned on Japan. The action was getting nearer, with the American assault on the islands in the Philippines, but those islands were about two thousand miles away from Singapore.

The Japanese must have heard about the fall of Germany, because Takahashi, the camp commandant, was making allusions to the war. Such information spread rapidly throughout the camp, and his cryptic remarks became known as 'Takahashi – he say'. Reference to the difficulties of surrender by the Japanese came as the Chinese proverb, 'He who rides the tiger cannot dismount'. An attempt to be friendly would appear as another Chinese saying, 'Beneath the four seas all men are brothers'. Takahashi obviously realized the war was approaching an end – with defeat for Japan – and he appeared to be building up goodwill between himself and the POWs. He could not go too far with his friendliness because his superiors were not of like mind. There was a general feeling of restlessness in the camp, with liberation appearing almost in our grasp. This feeling was enhanced by the news of the celebrations in Britain, and accompanied by doubts as to whether the fighting out East would be forgotten in the relief at the war ending in Europe.

We knew that the XIVth Army in Burma had been called 'The Forgotten Army' and suspected we might be the forgotten theatre of war. In June the news came that an attack had been made by Australian forces on Balikpapan, on the west coast of Borneo. There were oil wells there and we could see that the Allies were attempting to deny oil supplies to the Japanese. Balikpapan was also only about five hundred miles from Singapore, so war activity was coming closer.

The Australian forces next landed in British North Borneo, now called Sabah. The delight at hearing this news was tempered by the information about the POWs there; two contingents had gone from the regiment to Borneo early in 1943. We had been informed of their destination by the Japanese, so I had a personal interest in the news. When the Australians landed, the POWs in Sabah were taken on a forced march to prevent them being released by the attacking force. Many had died from this forced march and the remainder had eventually been released when the Australians caught up with the Japanese.

Our position in Singapore was then considered carefully. Where could we be forced to march from Singapore, if a landing was made on the island? If the mainland was attacked, would we be taken off in boats? We had heard on the news, months before, that several ships containing POWs bound for Japan had been sunk, and the prisoners on board had all been drowned.

After the landings on Borneo the news became quiet, and we were left wondering where the next assault would be. Then one day, two Allied planes flew over the camp. They were identified as Lightnings, with apparently two fuselages leading to two tail planes and with the cockpit in a nacelle between the fuselages. The planes flew over the camp, circled round it and then flew off. This was a cheering sight; the Australians now knew where the POW camp was located and we hoped it would not be bombed as a Japanese troop camp.

The Americans had been carrying out landings on the Japanese-occupied islands of the Philippines and they landed on an island called Palawan, the nearest island to the coast of Borneo.

The news of Okinawa and Iwojima had been of interest because the American forces were approaching the Japanese mainland. We hoped that the war out East would end with an attack on the mainland and with all the occupied areas in South East Asia then surrendering. This would be a safer bet for us to be released unharmed.

The news from Palawan, however, was the worst to date. When the American forces liberated the POW camp, they found that all the POWs had been burnt to death, and none had survived. Here was a second scenario for us to contemplate – march or burn. Perhaps it would have been better not to have heard the news; it only increased our anxieties.

One and all started to inspect the camp area very thoroughly, trying to make a plan for the various contingencies. The guards were too few to deal with the six or seven thousand prisoners in the camp, so presumably any Japanese troops in Singapore would be brought out to Changi to deal with the situation. The burning scenario was doubtful as it would entail all POWs concentrated in the gaol, and that would not burn very easily, being very solid stone.

So, on the whole, we thought that a march up country was going to be the answer, and we correspondingly made plans for an escape under such circumstances. Meanwhile, there was hardly any news of activity on any of the Eastern fronts. Burma was quiet, there was no further activity towards Japan, and Borneo seemed to have died down.

It was the middle of July and the war seemed to be suspended. The news came from Britain that Churchill had lost the election and that Britain now had a socialist government. This news was given a mixed reception, because most of us would have liked Churchill to keep on directing the British efforts to regain Malaya. The camp was in a state of suspended animation, not foreseeing the next direction of the war.

# CHAPTER XVII

# Oh Joseph, Joseph, won't you make your mind up

About the beginning of August 1945, there was a report on the news saying that a huge bomb had been dropped on Hiroshima on the mainland of Japan. Interest was expressed, but not more than usual because Japan had been bombed before now, and no details were given in this first mention of the bombing. The next bulletin, however, gave more details, and we learnt for the first time that it was an atomic bomb and had caused widespread damage.

More details still were given in the next news broadcast and it appeared that Hiroshima had been completely devastated – coupled with a demand for the Japanese to surrender unconditionally. This was an outcome that the POWs in the camp had hoped would be the course of action. If Japan surrendered, then there was no danger of reprisals on the POWs in the camps scattered throughout South East Asia.

Some time around the beginning of August the camp was informed by the camp commandant that all entertainment, courses, and other activities were to cease, although no reason was given. This was followed by working parties being detailed to unload fifty-gallon oil drums, all obviously full; they were brought to the camp and stored in the gaol. Remembering the fate of the POWs on Palawan, the arrival of the oil drums filled everyone with dread. It looked as if the alternative of burning and not marching was now on the agenda.

The alarm caused by the presence of the oil drums in the camp was increased when the camp was informed that men and officers were going to be separated. The men would remain in the gaol, and the officers would go to another camp, not specified. Other officers and men anywhere on the island, were to be brought back to these two locations. Activity on the part of the Japanese then seemed to die down and we heard nothing more about such a move.

There was no further news of events taking place in America or Japan, and once again there was an air of anticipation in the camp, tinged with some dread. Sometime around 10 August came the news of the bombing of Nagasaki, using an atomic bomb again. This was followed by an ultimatum from the Allies, we gathered, to the Japanese to surrender.

Once again there followed a period of waiting to see what action would be taken by the Japanese government. In the meantime, no action was being taken in the camp, the normal routine prevailed except that all entertainment was still cancelled. Then came the news for which we were eagerly waiting – the Japanese had surrendered. However, it was decided in the camp not to show any jubilation, in case the Japanese guards lost their temper. It was just as well that this decision was taken as there was a certain amount of activity on the part of the Japanese guards, although no information was given to the POWs.

The date for surrender was set for the fifteenth of August, and then we heard the news that General Saito had decided he was not going to surrender, but was going to defend the South East Asian Co-Prosperity Sphere to the end. He would maintain the honour of a Japanese officer and would never acknowledge defeat; he would rather commit ceremonial suicide. We had a nasty feeling that the POWs might be included in the suicide.

Gloom descended on the camp. The POWs had survived so much hardship up until now that to be placed in this situation seemed very unfair. We heard on the news that the UK was celebrating VJ day on the fifteenth of August, although the celebrations seemed a little less enthusiastic than those for VE day. We did not feel like joining in the celebrations, and wondered if the people in Europe knew of our predicament.

A week or so after VJ day the camp was still in a state of inactivity. The Japanese soldiers appeared to be getting Singapore island ready to be defended, and there was no news of any attempt to stop General Saito from carrying on with his plan. Then came the news that the Japanese government had ordered Saito to surrender, and it appeared that he might capitulate on receiving the Imperial orders.

The next day Saito repeated that he was not prepared to surrender and would defend the South East Asian Co-Prosperity Sphere. This alternation of raising our hopes and then dashing them was proving rather wearing, and we wished he would make his mind up. Then we heard on the news that the Japanese government had sent Prince Chichibu, a member of the Imperial family, to remonstrate with General Saito. So our hopes were once more raised.

Two or three days elapsed with nothing new happening, and then came the news that General Saito had agreed to the surrender. To confirm this, leaflets were dropped on the camp just before the end of August, telling us what to do now that the war was over. We were told to stay in our camps and make lists of the items that were most needed. The pamphlet also contained a warning not to overeat, as this would be harmful after such a long period of near starvation.

With the arrival of the pamphlets the Japanese started to release the Red Cross parcels that they had kept in store for months. These parcels were very welcome, and we took the advice of not eating or smoking too much. Life was becoming better day by day, and we now looked forward to being released from the camp.

The guards no longer guarded the camp and, theoretically, we were free to wander out. As we had no money and Singapore town was a long way away, there was not much point, so we just stayed where we were, following the advice in the pamphlet. As September began the Japanese seemed as confused as we were and they too stayed in their houses.

At this time the first members of RAPWI were dropped by parachute. RAPWI was an organization with the title 'Repatriation of Allied Prisoners of War and Internees', and the members of this organization had arrived to start the process of evacuation of all prisoners and internees. When we first saw them, clad in jungle green uniform, our impression was how fat they all were. Actually they were normal, and it was we who were very thin in comparison.

One or two of the more adventurous POWs, who had local connections, set off for Singapore and managed to reach the town. They went to the harbour and saw the Royal Navy fleet anchored there, with some vessels tied up to the wharf. One of the boats on the wharf was the light cruiser, the *Essex*, and the POWs were invited on board. The crew had many questions for them because they had heard in the UK just how badly the POWs had been treated.

As a final gesture of friendship the ship's crew gave the POWs a sack of bread, which they managed to carry back to the camp, late in the evening. This was a great treat, as none of us had eaten European bread for three and a half years. We had some Red Cross butter to go with it and enjoyed a magnificent supper. We were careful not to eat too much at one sitting, though, remembering the advice given in the pamphlet.

But not all the POWs heeded the warning about European food, and some of them ate too much. Three men each consumed a pound of butter because they were so delighted to get European food again. They died the next day, and everyone then heeded the warning. It seemed such a waste to be on the point of being released and then to die from overeating.

The Japanese guards had by this time been withdrawn from the camp and members of RAPWI entered and established a headquarters for dealing with the release of the prisoners. Their office had an immense amount of organization to set up. As the POWs were no longer in military units, there was no suitable record of personnel in the camp. The first step in arranging the evacuation was to find out the names, numbers, and units of all the POWs. This was done hut by hut until all had been recorded.

The first journalist to arrive was a very pretty New Zealand female reporter. She came into the camp and called to those POWs she could see. As we approached her she said 'Gather round, boys, and let me have your news and views'. This we did, but when we got within five feet of her we recoiled. She was obviously puzzled and asked, 'What's the matter, why don't you come closer?'

One bold spirit from the back of the crowd called out 'You smell', an answer that amazed her, so she asked, 'What do I smell of?' Having a well trained chemist's nose I replied tentatively, 'You smell like the lion's cage in the zoo, liberally sprinkled with Chanel No. 5 and it's a ghastly combination'.

This made her laugh and she replied, 'I may smell but I'm afraid you stink.' Having got over these pleasantries we started to answer her questions. She was interested in the work we had been doing, the conditions in the camps, and most interested in the working parties on the Burma–Siam railway. She made notes for about an hour and we hoped she then had a good account of life in the various POW camps.

The question and answer on the aspect of smell interested me. When we first arrived in Malaya we were warned not to go too close to a water buffalo, as if we did, the buffalo would put its head down and charge, making a hasty retreat necessary. However, little local boys could go up to the water buffalo, flick it on the nose and the beast would move away.

When working up in Thailand we had come across the odd water buffalo and, to our surprise, the animal took no notice of us. In fact we could then go up to it and also flick it on the nose. The rice diet had made a difference to the way we smelt, and we obviously no longer smelt like carnivores. The New Zealand reporter had smelt just like a carnivore, hence the description of the lion's den.

Clothing had arrived in the camp and we attended the RAPWI quartermaster's store to receive the first issue of proper clothing since we had been made prisoners. The issue was the jungle green tropical clothing, a surprise to us because previously our clothing had been khaki. We were issued with underwear, also green, with cellular singlets and pants; bush shirts and trousers completed the kit. Also included was a kitbag to contain spare clothing and other necessities.

The relief at being properly clad for the first time for ages was immense. For shoes we had the Indian *chaplis*, sandals with a strap round the ankle. For hats we had the soft variety known as 'giggle hats'. Other items, such as a cleaning kit, including razors and blades, were also issued.

Having a new razor and blades was very acceptable, as I, and many others, had existed on three blades for three and a half years. To sharpen the blades we used marmite jars, obtained from Red Cross parcels and medical stores. By wetting the inside of the jar and rubbing the blade around it, it could be honed to some degree of satisfaction. Officers had been ordered to shave as well as possible during the whole of our captivity, but by the end the blades were getting somewhat blunt, and shaving was not a pleasant experience.

The last stage of this period was a medical examination, beginning with the POWs in hospital. All the men classified as fit were then examined for fitness to travel. We were informed that those POWs who were fit would return to England at the earliest possible opportunity, while those who were too sick to travel far would go to India to be treated in hospital.

Whilst all the activity of being clothed and medically examined was going on, information was requested on our treatment during captivity. The request was mainly aimed at reporting atrocities or general maltreatment, but, at the same time, information on any good aspects of treatment was sought.

I decided, and then wrote, about the beneficial behaviour of Oburi *gunso*. Because he had been in charge of POW camps, I suspected he would be interrogated – and perhaps blamed under the general opprobrium towards all such camp commanders. My comments, I hoped, would stand him in good stead should the need arise. Later, trying to get information on the lower ranking members of the military was difficult, and I never found out what happened to Oburi *gunso*. I wish I had.

During the whole of my captivity – and the same treatment was given to others – I had been allowed to send home only three cards, each containing a maximum of twenty-five words, including the address. This did not leave much room for a message, but the cards were duly written and handed back to the Japanese, and from them supposedly went to the Red Cross for onward transmission.

The RAPWI officials now gave us cards to fill in for sending home, which we did with enthusiasm. However, when I did eventually reach England, I found that none of the cards – either those sent by the Japanese, or those sent by RAPWI – ever reached their destination. Even after a month or so, nothing had arrived, and where they all went was never discovered.

We were about to embark on the last stage – bound for England. All that remained was to decide in what order we would go, and who went to England, and who went to India.

# CHAPTER XVIII

# It's been a long, long time

Having been made presentable with our new clothing and been medically examined, we waited for the instructions to begin the voyage home. The first list of six hundred fit officers and men was posted, and I found I was on the list. Transport was provided by lorries, more comfortable than the Japanese lorries used on the previous trips, and the convoy started off for Singapore harbour.

We arrived on one of the wharfs of the harbour and embarked on the S.S. *Monowai*, a medium-sized steam ship of the New Zealand Shipping Line. There were members of RAPWI on board, together with a medical contingent of doctors and nurses. The RAPWI officials organized the accommodation as we boarded the ship.

The officers were accommodated in cabins, the ship having been altered from its peacetime layout of a passenger liner to that of a troopship. A cabin held between six and twelve officers according to its size, with double bunks.

After being allotted a cabin and having selected a bunk, most of us went on deck to see the activity going on along the wharf. Rice, unloaded from ships tied up to the wharf was being stacked in godowns. There was a constant stream of military traffic with vehicles of all sizes, and for the first time we saw a jeep. Inquiries from passers-by gave the information that food was being provided for the civilian population, under the command of the British Military Authority.

We had arrived on board in the middle of the morning and had to wait for the rest of the POWs and the internees to come aboard. Our first meal was lunch, and it consisted entirely of European food, our introduction to the pattern of feeding for the rest of the trip. We enjoyed the meal – perhaps lacking in taste after some of the fiercer oriental flavours – and it was accompanied by half a pint of beer. The medical staff in charge of our diet gradually increased the quantity of beer during the voyage to England.

The remainder of the POWs arrived after lunch and the civilian internees during the afternoon. The *Monowai* sailed just before sunset on 10 September and, as we steamed out of the harbour, all the naval vessels saluted the ship with their sirens. We stood on deck listening to the noise of the salutation, and waved farewell to sunny Singapore.

Dinner was served and with it we started a course of mepacrin to make sure that any malarial parasites in our blood were eliminated before we reached England. We were given mepacrin at dinner and at breakfast, and the dose was large enough to eventually turn our skin yellow. By the time we reached England most of us looked like foreigners, with the combination of exposure to the sun and the dose of mepacrin.

Steaming up the Malacca Straits we observed a lot of mine-sweeping in progress, and heard that sweeping the Straits had only just begun. The mine-sweeping fleet was forming a narrow channel for marine traffic. Although we did not know it at the time, the invasion of Malaya was going ahead as planned at Port Dickson and was another reason for the mine-sweeping activity. On this first day of the voyage the internees began complaining about their accommodation.

Whether intentionally or by accident, the internees had chosen the sickest six hundred of their number to board the first boat. So we had the fittest POWs and the sickest internees, with the internees down in the hold, the officers in cabins and the troops in mess decks. The RAPWI officer in charge of the ship's company had to mollify the internees, and he finally accepted their complaint that there were six internees with heart trouble.

These six internees said they could not manage all the companion ways from the hold to the saloon on the upper deck, and the doctors of the RAPWI group agreed. The doctors decided to exchange the six sick internees with the six fittest officers, so we were once again medically examined to find the six really fit officers. I found myself in that group of six, so was banished from my cabin down into the hold on F deck. I agreed with the internees, it was a stiff climb from F deck to the upper deck.

By the second day of our voyage, we began to feel the effects of a European diet; we found it indigestible and it settled in our stomachs like a mass of concrete. We longed for some rice instead of potatoes, and we also became constipated.

Down in the hold I was becoming used to climbing into a hammock without falling out on the other side. But I did not particularly like sleeping in a hammock, especially when you looked over the side to see where you had left your shoes. The shoes, underneath the hammock, swung in an arc to and fro, and the sight of this was enough to make anyone seasick.

The six officers down in the hold formed a special group, with a lively detestation of internees. It was not easy to keep up with the happenings in the officers mess on the upper deck, and we felt a trifle isolated, although being accommodated in the hold did stand us in good stead when we reached Colombo, which we did after sunset on the fifth day. As we entered the harbour, boats with searchlights turned on their lights to form the letter V in the sky, making a terrific display. All boats sounded their sirens, and any other form of klaxons, and kept the sounds of celebration going for about an hour and a half.

It was a welcome that was completely unexpected, and made us feel like VIPs. We had dinner and stood on the boat deck for some time, looking at Colombo, and trying to realize that Singapore finally lay behind us.

The next day outings appeared to have been arranged for all of the POWs, but we had missed out, because of our lateness in reaching the mess. Actually this was good, because a group of Wren officers came on board, looking for a party of officers. The six of us from the hold were grabbed as trophies and triumphantly transported to the Wren mess in Colombo.

In the mess we were questioned and entertained for lunch. The six of us were rather quiet, as there had been no contact with female company for nearly four years, and we had difficulty in maintaining a conversation. The Wrens were kind and helped us out by chattering away about life in Ceylon. In the afternoon we were taken on a sight-seeing and shopping expedition in the town and delivered back to the boat in time for tea.

Although the Wrens were kindness itself we did feel as though we were specimens that invited curiosity, rather like prize animals let out from the zoo. The Wrens who had captured us would probably be recounting their exploit to other envious naval personnel.

The boat left harbour early in the morning, so we did not see Colombo disappear over the horizon. We steamed to Aden where we took on oil and water – but were not allowed to go on shore – and then up the Red Sea to Suez. On the coast in the bay at Suez was a large army port in the charge of a Royal Engineer Dock Company.

We lay at anchor in the bay and officers of the Pay Corps came on the boat to give us some sterling, for which we signed against our future pay. In the afternoon we went ashore in groups, the officers to an officers' shop and the troops to the quartermaster's store. At the officers' shop we could buy clothing and uniforms for use in England.

The purchase of this clothing required a little thought as we needed every single item for a cold climate. Beginning with underwear, and moving on to battle dress, caps, and trench coats, all were purchased by signing a special POW army form. At the same time, we were given our medal ribbons; we requested those that we were entitled to from an information pamphlet on the award of medals.

Amongst the medals we could claim was the Pacific Star, and when we were given the ribbon we all laughed. It was yellow stripes on a green back ground, but not crossed running shoes in yellow as we had thought. Now, complete with uniform, medal ribbons, and some sterling, we were ready to face the cold climate in England. There had been no celebration of our arrival in Suez; all the ships were trying to get through the Suez canal as quickly as possible.

In Colombo we had heard how short transport was for troops leaving the East and bound for home. Besides troop ships, aircraft carriers were being used to speed up the transport of army and air force personnel from India. Our boat joined in the queue for the canal and, finally, we were away and steaming slowly to Port Said.

We did not linger at Port Said but sailed straight into the Mediterranean. It was getting towards the end of September, and all of us found the climate too cold for our liking. Having been in the tropics for over four years, most of us found it hard to acclimatize to the lower temperatures. The weather was sunny, so that was a comfort, and out of the wind it could be pleasantly warm. The next stop was Gibraltar, where we arrived in the morning, to be greeted by all ships sounding their sirens in welcome to us. We anchored in the bay, exchanged mail with the garrison there and three Wrens came to join the boat to be transported to England. The celebration was in honour of the S.S. *Monowai* being the first ship to call in at Gibraltar with ex-POWs aboard. We gathered that a second ship with ex-POWs was not far behind us.

We were now in October and the weather was much colder, with a rough sea in the Bay of Biscay. We were glad of our winter clothing and spent as much time on the boat deck as we could, usually chatting with the Wrens. After having lived for so long in outdoor conditions, or in huts which were almost like living outdoors, we found cabins and rooms claustrophobic, and wondered how we would survive English houses.

Finally we entered the Irish Sea, and steamed past the Welsh coast one afternoon. It was a dull, grey, overcast day, and the coast was a grey background on the horizon. We gazed at the gloomy land and the overcast sky, and said 'Turn the boat round, we're going back to sunny Singapore'.

We arrived at Liverpool late at night and had to tie up to the buoys at the mouth of the river, as the tide was too low for us to cross the bar. The ship did not sail until morning and we slowly steamed up the river to the landing stage. We were greeted by sirens on our arrival, but learnt that we had become the second ship to arrive in England. The ship which had been behind us had gone into Southampton and, not having to wait for the tide, had beaten us by a few hours.

There was a civic reception waiting for us on the landing stage, with the mayor of Liverpool in full regalia, together with other members of the corporation; they came on board to meet the POWs. After they had departed, a late lunch was served and arrangements for us to land were made.

Transport was becoming more civilized and we left the landing stage in a convoy of coaches. The weather had worsened and there was a fine drizzle – which did not improve the look of the streets in Liverpool. As we drove through the town, they were lined with the local inhabitants. The drive was made in silence and we had the impression that we were objects of curiosity, rather than objects of celebration.

We arrived at an army camp some distance from Liverpool and were shown into huts where we would spend the night. A battery of telephones had been installed by the Post Office, and all of us could make as many telephone calls as we wanted, free of charge, to anywhere in Great Britain.

We queued for use of the telephones, and I contacted my family early in the evening. The family was very surprised to hear me; they had had no news from me since just before the Japanese attacked Malaya. Moreover, they had had a communication just before the fall of Singapore to say that I was missing. This had happened because the battery had been cut off by the Japanese advance and was behind the front line. Malaya command had then reported the personnel of the battery as missing.

When we did manage to rejoin the fight in Singapore town, it was too late to send confirmation that we were no longer missing. Hence the family had known that I was missing in February 1942 and had had no further news until I telephoned from Liverpool.

The next day we were given train tickets and despatched home to wait for further orders. And so we went home – most of the POWs having been away from England for about five years.

# CHAPTER XIX

# Epilogue

Not long after I had arrived home, a letter came from the War Office to tell me that a club had been formed for ex-POWs from the Far East, and giving the address. We were asked to contact the club, so I went up to London and joined. The accommodation was not yet complete, but the organization had started – with the primary aim of seeking and dispensing information.

The most important part of this aim was the tracing of POWs still listed as missing, having not been traced by RAPWI. The secondary aim was to provide information to POWs of events that might interest them, and bring them into closer contact with people in England.

It may sound strange that POWs could be described as missing, but records had ceased to be kept when military units were split up. The regiment to which I belonged had the majority of officers and men sent to Japan, and most of the remainder dispersed to other countries. Officers who were my particular friends had been sent as far apart as Mukden in Manchuria, Kyushu – one of the Japanese islands – and Borneo; others, like me, had been in Thailand. None had remained in Singapore. It was thus not possible to keep complete records of the unit as a whole. I was partially aware of the fate of the eighty or so troops of the regiment who had originally been in Changi village and in the hospital area, prior to my group going to Thailand. Of the fifty-one men who had gone with me to Thailand, I had first hand, second-hand, and even some third-hand news of the thirty-four who had died up country. Those few who had become detached from the rest of the contingent were known to have died, but the place where they died, and the cause of death, were unknown. About the rest of the regiment, who had left Changi before me, I had no knowledge.

Such facts as I did have were given to the staff of the POWs' club and recorded on their information lists. These lists showed at least the location where a person was last known to be and, hopefully, greater detail of his circumstances. Anybody tracing a missing relative might eventually track down other POWs who had been at that location and who might supply further information.

Thinking of my trip from Nikki down to Kanburi, the men who had died on that trip were unknown to me and neither their name nor unit could be recorded. There must have been many similar situations occurring during the building of the railway, with no records left of POWs who had died in isolated circumstances such as these. All such incidents led to the lack of information concerning the fate of many prisoners and resulted in the list of missing POWs.

The club provided a valuable meeting place for ex-POWs where we could talk about our experiences. Most of us had found difficulty in reconciling ourselves to life in England, because we felt strangely alienated from the civilian population and even from many service people. We had experiences in common with service people who had served overseas, but little in common with service people who had spent the war in Britain.

Our experience of a totally different foreign culture had altered our views on life, and we could find little sympathy with some of the current socialist views of the British people. This caused most POWs to withdraw from close contact with their previous circle of friends, some being affected more than others. Some withdrew from social contact altogether, while others – realizing that England had almost become a foreign country – decided to go abroad; others became restless and departed from home.

Many communities organized special parties for the ex-POWs and I was invited to one of them. There were three ex-POWs at the party, one from Germany, one from Italy, and me from the Far East. It was an enjoyable evening and two people approached me to find out where they could get information regarding missing relatives who had served in Malaya. I took them to the POW club, and put them in contact with the staff.

There was a special treat for the POWs; we were all given bananas. This must have entailed a considerable sacrifice on the part of the organizers, because bananas were scarcer than gold dust at that time. I could hardly tell the people that bananas had been part of my diet. It was incidents such as this that made former POWs of the Japanese realize how difficult it was to bridge the gap between conditions in England and in the tropics. As time went on, we became aware of the lack of interest in England for events and conditions in distant countries; this lack of interest is still apparent.

★ ★ ★

In conclusion, some extra points of interest have come to light through newspaper articles, and some personal contacts.

From the articles I read about a camp at Kranji for sick people, and the arrival there of the surgeon I had assisted in Kanchanaburi. I was glad he had survived and had gone on to have a successful career in Australia – even though the information came in an obituary. This news could also explain why we had no amputees at Sime Road camp; they had probably all gone, under the surgeon's jurisdiction, to Kranji.

The next item of news concerned Robert, my fellow officer who had given me the tin of water in Kanchanaburi. After the war, Robert had gone back to his firm in India, and had come on a short visit to Malaya. He looked me up in Malacca and we had a get together. We then lost contact until I was given his telephone number in 1995. We had several conversations, but did not meet again. He was partially blind, due to adverse treatment by the guards and from the poor food in the camps. Unfortunately, he died a year and a half after I had made contact – the last of the POWs from my regiment that I knew.

The last item of news concerned my friend Bill, who had taught me Thai. I had often wondered why I had not been allowed to go with him to Siam, and I found out the possible explanation. When I had seen Bill in Kanchanaburi he was obviously on a buying expedition with the local traders, and had come from Chungkai. On his buying trips he had made contact with Thais, and through them, with his Chinese friends. He started to send information through the Chinese, eventually getting it to Burma and then India. He then set up an information network supplying India with information concerning the Japanese activities in Siam. Bill had never mentioned this to me, so presumably it was still confidential information just after the war. As it is now fifty or more years since his activities were operational, any such information is obviously now out of date, but I have never seen any account of this aspect of the war in the Far East.

# Death Under the Rising Sun

At the start of POW life in Changi, accurate statistics of all personnel were kept, but as the war progressed, statistics of prisoners in Singapore and Malaya became chaotic. Both large and small groups from Changi were dispersed to Japan, Thailand, and Borneo, and some were sent even as far as Mukden in Manchuria. The large groups were often split into small groups, and such groups had no organization for keeping accurate records of personnel.

According to government sources, 193,000 Allied personnel (British, Australian and Indian) were taken prisoner in the Pacific theatre of war. Of these Allied POWs, 60,500 died in various military camps. A further 600,000 troops of other nationalities, including those of Far Eastern nationalities, became POWs and of these 290,000 died in captivity.

50,000 POWs of the Allied forces were British, and 12,500 died in military camps, a much higher death rate than in European POW camps. In Malaya, from a total force of 138,000, 130,000 were taken prisoner.

The number of POWs taken into Changi, at the surrender of Singapore, was 51,000, and these consisted of British and Australian troops. The remainder were Indian troops, some of whom joined the Indian National Army (INA), fighting for Japan. Those Indian troops who did not join the INA were prisoners in other military camps, or were working on the Burma-Siam railway.

During 1942, POWs came to Changi from the Dutch East Indies – including British as well as Dutch troops and also a few Americans from naval losses. Prisoners were also dispatched in groups from Changi to other countries, including Thailand, before the end of the year. Although the POWs in Changi consisted of a mixture of nationalities, any group leaving the camp generally consisted of one nationality only.

From January to March 1943 F and H Forces, numbering 10,000 men, were sent in groups of 600 to Thailand to speed up the construction of the Burma-Siam railway. The two forces were made up of British and Australian troops.

Previous forces, including a medical group labelled K force, had already been sent up to Thailand to start building the railway. These forces, together with F and H Forces, probably totalled about 18,000 men, British and Australian.

During 1943, our camp in Tonchan South was reinforced with troops from the Dutch army to replace losses from cholera, malaria and tropical ulcers. About 300 of the 600 men had died, or had been incapacitated by ulcers and evacuated to base camps down the railway.

When the two Tonchan camps were eventually broken up, the prisoners were dispersed to other camps, higher up the railway. When I arrived at Nikki, near the Burmese border, I worked with British, Australian, and Dutch troops, and even with nationals from the Far East, some of whom were from civilian work forces.

Estimates of deaths amongst workers on the Burma-Siam railway were 6,500 British, 9,500 Commonwealth (Australian and Indian) troops, and 80,000 other nationalities. The other nationalities may have included some civilian workers.

F and H Forces accounted for at least 6,000 POWs who died in Thailand, with a further 600 dying in Singapore, after the two forces had been evacuated from Thailand to Singapore. The death rate of British prisoners in Thailand was almost twice as great as in other areas of the Far East.

Official estimates★ also indicate that the death rate of British prisoners in the Far East was five times greater than in German camps.

---

★ See: *Prisoners of the Rising Sun* by Graham N. Thompson

# Glossary

**Agar** (*Mal*)    Vegetable gelatin, prepared from a type of seaweed.

**Assam fork**    A four-pronged fork attached to a haft at right angles, useful for breaking up ground.

**Atap** (*Mal*)    Narrow palm leaves, bent double round a bamboo rod, forming a fringe of about six inches. The rod is about five feet long, and when the rods are placed one above the other, spaced at about two inches, they form a thatch to a roof. This thatch is also called an *atap*, and provides excellent protection against all types of weather.

**Battalion**    In the British army, composed of four companies, and a headquarter company, of infantry.

**Battery**    In 1940 a battery consisted of three troops, each of which had four guns. After 1940, a battery consisted of two troops, each of which had four guns.

**Belachan** (Mal)    Matured prawn paste, with a cheesy, fishy taste.

**Brigade**    An army unit with three infantry battalions, and one artillery regiment. Brigades operating on their own usually had attached units of engineers, ordnance corps, and service corps.

**Butt**    The end part of a rifle, held against the shoulder when firing.

**Byoki** (*Jap*)    Ill, or sick.

**Chang** (*Thai*)    A low platform made from flattened, split bamboos, supported on bamboo legs, about two to three feet high.

**Changkol** (*Mal*)    A small spade attached to a haft at right angles, very useful for digging, better than an English spade.

**Chapli** (*Urdu*)    A sandal with overlapping uppers from each side held by a strap at the back.

**Desu** (*Jap*)    Am, is, are

**Desukah** (*Jap*)    The *kah* at the end of a word forms a question; am, is, are?

**Frond**    The leaf of a palm tree, growing out of a mid-rib.

| | |
|---|---|
| **Gunso** (*Jap*) | A sergeant in the Japanese army. |
| **Gun trail** | A gun, or a howitzer, consists of a barrel – with a buffer-recuperator system which takes the recoil and returns the barrel to its rest position, and a trail. The trail rests on the ground, and connects to the axle between the two wheels of the gun. The barrel and the buffer system are joined to the trail at the axle. At the end of the trail is a spade that digs into the ground when the gun is fired. |
| **Howitzer** | A cannon that fires at a greater elevation than a gun to reach the same target distance. A 4.5 howitzer has a calibre of 4.5 inches; two shells, in their wooden case for carrying, weigh about 100 pounds. |
| **Ikan** (*Mal*) | A fish, or fish plural. |
| **INA** | Indian National Army. Indian troops serving in the Japanese army, having deserted from the British forces. |
| **Kampong** (*Mal*) | A Malay village – quite unlike an English village – as there is no particular road system associated with it, and the houses are placed higgledy-piggledy over the area. |
| **Karma** (*San*) | The soul of any living human or animal. When the human or animal dies, the soul is transferred to another human or animal. |
| **Kempei-tai** (*Jap*) | The intelligence branch of the Japanese army, the equivalent of the Gestapo for the German army. |
| **Klong** (*Thai*) | A canal running through towns, settled areas, and even open country. Bangkok has many *klongs*, similar (in construction) to the canals in Venice. |
| **Kota** (*Mal*) | A fort, a town. |
| **Kuala** (*Mal*) | A river mouth at the sea, or the mouth of a tributary into a main river. |
| **Kuali** (*Mal*) | A cooking utensil, called a wok in England. The *kualis* used in camp were about three feet in diameter. |
| **Lagi** (*Mal*) | More, in addition; the Malay word, *lebeh*, means 'more than', as in the phrase more than a hundred dollars'. If you have one hundred dollars, and are given twenty more, this is *lagi* twenty. |
| **Malay Volunteer Force** | Army units, similar to the units of the Territorial Army, with volunteers of all races from the civilian population. |
| **MVF** | Malay Volunteer Force. |
| **Oru** (*Jap*) | The nearest the Japanese could get to pronouncing 'all'. There is no letter 'l' in the Japanese language, so it is pronounced as the letter 'r'. Japanese words end with a vowel, unless the word ends in 'n', 'ng', or 'm'. |

| | |
|---|---|
| **Padang** (*Mal*) | An open space, frequently covered in grass, used for sports and ceremonies. |
| **Pungkis** (*Mal*) | A cane basket, in the shape of a shovel, with slightly raised back and sides, with two carrying handles, one on each side. It could carry about 30–40 pounds of earth. |
| **RAPWI** | Repatriation of Allied Prisoners of War and Internees. A branch of the army concerned with army and civilian personnel on the cessation of hostilities. |
| **Rattan** | A type of thin cane that can be used to weave a basket. |
| **Regiment** | An artillery regiment consisted of two batteries in 1940, but became three batteries after 1940. Whether two or three batteries, the total number of guns was 24, but our regiment had only 16 guns in two batteries. |
| **Shoko** (*Jap*) | An officer. |
| **Skip** | A basket of palm leaves stiffened with bamboo, circular in shape, about 3½ feet deep, with a diameter of about three feet. A bamboo pole was passed through holes near the top of the basket, and the pole was carried on the shoulders of two men. |
| **Tanjong** (*Mal*) | A cape, or a bend in a river. |
| **Tenko** (*Jap*) | Roll call. |
| **Terompak** (*Mal*) | A flip-flop shoe with a wooden sole, and a canvas, or rubber, band for gripping the foot. In common use all over Asia. |
| **Tong** (*Chi*) | A large earthenware jar, about three or four feet tall. |
| **Trail** | *See* gun trail. |
| **Troop** | A unit of an artillery battery, with four guns. A battery was composed of two or three troops. |
| **Urdu** | The language used in the Indian Army. As there are over 200 different languages in India, a common language has to be learned by all troops in order to communicate efficiently. |
| **Wang** (*Mal*) | Money, as in *wang pisang*, banana money, with *pisang* the word for banana. |
| **Yasmi** (*Jap*) | Rest; both the actual state, and an army command (stand at ease). |

# Acknowledgements

I must thank Kinn Mcintosh for reading my original typescript and for making so many helpful suggestions. It was largely her confidence in my book that inspired me to complete it.

I must also thank the two distinguished artists, Philip Meninsky and Ronald Searle – both fellow prisoners – who have generously provided the illustrations which are such an important part of the book. Philip Meninsky's drawings were buried, inserted in bamboo and wrapped in gas cape, in old ammunition boxes. When the war finished he returned and dug them out. Both artists' drawings are now housed in the Imperial War Museum, London. Jennifer Wood of the Department of Art, IWM, and Camilla Roberts of the Tessa Sayle Agency have been most helpful in arranging for the illustrations to be made available.

# About the Artists

## PHILIP MENINSKY

Philip Meninsky was born in London, the younger son of painter and art teacher Bernard Meninsky, and brought up in Hertfordshire. Leaving school shortly before the outbreak of World War II, he joined his County Regiment and was sent to the Far East. Captured after the fall of Singapore, he was sent to forced labour on the Siam-Burma railway, where he met Ronald Searle.

During his period of captivity and immediately afterwards, he made drawings for the Australian medical authorities, many of which were used in the trials of war criminals, and 70 of which are now in the collection of the Imperial War Museum.

After the war, Philip Meninsky settled in Scotland, where he met his wife Elaine, and became associated with Glasgow School of Art. He began to exhibit regularly and, in 1961, he had his first one-man exhibition under the auspices of the Scottish Arts Council.

His work is found in many private collections in Russia, North America, Western Europe and Britain, including that of HRH The Duke of Edinburgh. It is based firmly in the figurative tradition and on a conviction that mastery of life drawing is an essential pre-requisite of all painting and drawing of worth. His mastery of the human form has led him to develop a specialisation in the work of the stage.

He was commissioned by London Weekend Television to draw studies of Francesca Annis as Lillie Langtry for the award-winning series *Lillie*. In 1981, he began to work with Masque Dance Theatre, then with the London Festival Ballet (now English National Ballet), resulting in several exhibitions of his studies of dancers.

Philip Meninsky was made 'appointed artist' to the English National Ballet School in 1990. He was drawing and painting every day almost to the end of his life. Philip Meninsky died in 2007.

## RONALD SEARLE

Ronald Searle's artistic career began in 1935 at the age of fifteen, as weekly cartoonist to a Cambridge local paper. The money helped to pay for his studies at Cambridge School of Art, which he left with a precocious grasp of the technical problems of drawing.

In April 1939, while still at art college, he volunteered for the army. In September 1939 he was called up and two years later he embarked for Singapore where, a month after his arrival, he found himself a prisoner of the Japanese. After fourteen months in a prisoner-of-war camp he was sent north – to a work camp on the Burma Railway. Half-starved, debilitated by exhaustion and disease, Searle and his comrades struggled to build a railway that has since been swallowed up by the jungle. In May 1944 he was sent to his last destination as a prisoner: Changi Gaol in Singapore, a prison constructed for 600 prisoners into which the Japanese crammed five thousand.

Throughout his captivity Ronald Searle made drawings, determined – despite the risk – to record his experiences. He drew his fellow prisoners and his Japanese guards; he sketched places and people glimpsed while on the move; he recorded significant events – the triumphant Japanese entering Singapore, the planes dropping leaflets announcing the end of the war. Stained with the sweat and dirt of forty years ago, the drawings are a remarkable record of one man's war, what Ronald Searle calls 'the graffiti of a condemned man, intending to leave a rough witness of his passing through, but who found himself— to his surprise and delight – among the reprieved'.

He went on to gain international acclaim as a 'black' humourist with what Max Beerbohm called 'a power to convert the macabre into the most pleasurable of frolics', *St Trinian's* included. He has been a major influence on succeeding generations of graphic artists, both in Europe and America, where, as Tom Wolfe wrote, he is considered a 'giant of the graphic netherworld'.

Ronald Searle left England in 1961. After many years in Paris, he spent the following decades in a mountain village in the foothills of the Alps of Provence, with his wife Monica, who is also an artist. In 2007 he was awarded the Légion d'Honneur.

Both Ronald Searle and Philip Meninsky created a prodigious amount of artwork, many thousands of pieces. The experiences they shared with Arthur Godman perhaps, in part, led to their later awe-inspiring productivity.